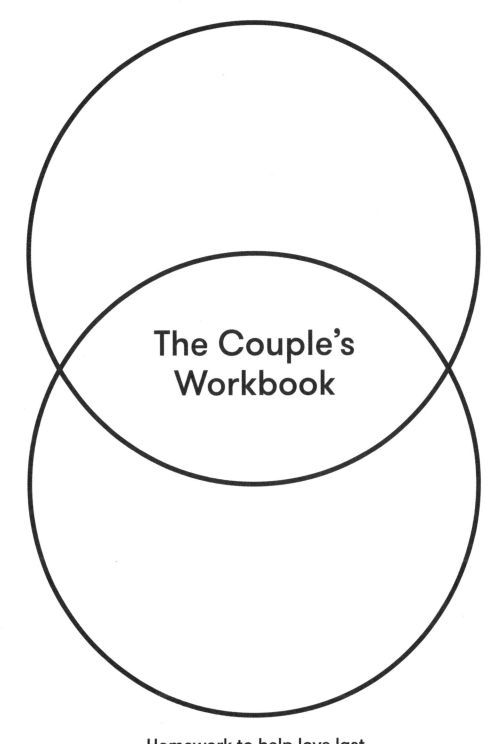

The Couple's Workbook

Homework to help love last

Published in 2020 by The School of Life
First published in the USA in 2021
70 Marchmont Street, London WC1N 1AB

Copyright © The School of Life 2020

Designed and typeset by Ryan Bartaby
Printed in Italy by Lego

A proportion of this book has appeared
online at theschooloflife.com/thebookoflife

Every effort has been made to contact
the copyright holders of the materials
reproduced in this book. If any have been
inadvertently overlooked, the publisher
will be pleased to make restitution at the
earliest opportunity.

The School of Life is a resource for helping
us understand ourselves, for improving
our relationships, our careers and our social
lives – as well as for helping us find calm
and get more out of our leisure hours. We do
this through creating films, workshops,
books and gifts.

www.theschooloflife.com

ISBN 978-1-912891-26-9

10 9 8 7 6 5 4 3

Introduction   4

The Pledge   6

1. The Scale of the Ambition   9

2. The Dangerous Quest   15
    for Compatibility

3. The True Romance of Pessimism   21

4. Why on Earth Am I   24
    With *This* Person?

5. What We Should Learn   32
    From One Another

6. The Secret Lives of   37
    Other Couples

7. Continuing the Conversation   42

8. Overcoming Our Parents   45

9. A Trust Check-Up   51

10. How We See Ourselves – And   56
    How Our Partner Sees Us

11. The Little Things   61

12. How We Like to Be Loved   70

13. Early Wounds   78

14. A New Ritual: The Morning   87
    and Evening Kiss

15. Unconscious Belittling   89

16. The Anxious-Avoidant Quiz   93

17. Projecting Emotions   97

18. Indirect Communication   103

19. A Better Kind of Evening   110

20. How I Am Difficult to Live With   114

21. A Forgiveness Ritual   117

22. A Gratitude Ritual   121

23. Our Conspiracy   124

24. Admiration   126

25. The Weakness of Strength   129

26. Hidden Efforts   134

27. Undelivered Compliments   138

28. How to Complain   143

29. A Pessimistic Interlude   150

30. How to Argue   154

31. Concrete Change   164

32. Change is Possible   166

33. Be the Change You   168
    Want to See

34. Five Questions to Ask   171
    of Bad Behaviour

35. Talking About Sex   174

36. The Sensate Focus Method   179

37. Accepting the Problems   181

38. Less Pressure on Love   183

Conclusion   188

Introduction

A great many tasks are obviously so tricky (landing a plane, overseeing a court case, extracting a tooth) that we have no qualms about accepting that we will have to train for a long time before we give them a go. However, significantly, we haven't yet added love to this list of ambitions that we would ideally need to train for. We've inherited a Romantic perspective that suggests that living successfully with another person – maybe for decades – only depends on two relatively straightforward details: finding 'the right person' and experiencing a high degree of mutual passion from the first.

Unfortunately, the results of this attitude have been disastrous. The great majority of relationships end in heartache within two to three years, while those that survive longer – and may lead to marriage – normally involve a sizeable amount of quiet suffering. Being deeply unhappy but undivorced is possibly the dominant state of most couples' existence. After a heady and passion-filled start, many of us end up in unions that are a confusing tangle of hope, distance, boredom, irritation, loyalty and betrayal. The added irony is that we tend to think that we're alone with our problems.

It's not strange that all of this should happen. Almost no one ever finds a person with whom they miraculously and intuitively connect across all areas. However compelling someone may appear to be at the outset, time almost inevitably reveals them as a bit maddening in multiple ways. Of course there are exceptional couples, but they are awe-inspiringly rare and generate a tragically misleading idea of what's likely to happen in our own case. We would be better off assuming from the outset that a relatively pronounced degree of pain and discord is going to be our lot.

We should graciously understand that being together in the long term is a fiendishly difficult project that requires us to submit to education. We're going to have to go back to school. Yet we should also maintain a faith that even if a relationship is currently very difficult, it's almost always open to being changed and improved in at least a few important areas – so long as we practise. Not every relationship can become ideal. But it is fair to suppose that the vast majority of them can end up being good enough: that is, relationships where, alongside a degree of friction and awkwardness, life can be broadly constructive, occasionally tender and sometimes delightful.

This workbook brings together a wide range of exercises that can help a couple to build mature communication, that foster understanding and that nurture patience, forgiveness, humour and resilience in the face of the many frustrations that attend any attempt to live with someone else. The notion of exercising is well understood in many areas – water skiing or French verbs, for example – and we should grant that it applies equally well to relationships. No one is intuitively good at love. We all need to do a little homework.

Through this book, we confront an odd but crucial thought: that love is a skill, not an emotion – and that we owe it to ourselves and our loved ones to undergo a few playful, intriguing and consoling exercises that can improve our capacity to be a good enough partner.

Instructions on how to fill in this book

Throughout these pages, you will find sections in two different colours:

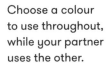

Choose a colour to use throughout, while your partner uses the other.

Take time to fill in as many of the exercises as feels comfortable.

The Pledge

The surest indicator of the success of a relationship is not whether or not there are arguments, moments of fury, stretches of loneliness or incidents of betrayal; it is – quite simply – whether or not two people want to be together.

If they do, and if they firmly know this of themselves and of the other, then pretty much every obstacle can be overcome. The fractious current state of a relationship is never enough to doom it. Saying in the heat of an argument that one hates one's partner and wishes to divorce them tomorrow morning (or worse) means nothing whatsoever. All that matters is the underlying concrete intention that one carries in one's heart and which – surprisingly – people often don't share either with their partner or with themselves … until it's too late.

Therefore, as a prelude to consulting any of the specific exercises in this book, we want you to consider whether or not you can sign up to a declaration. We are interested in intentions, not (yet) in action.

If you can sign up to these words, however many squabbles you may have had, however hard intimacy might be, however many bad words may have been said in fury, then half the battle at least has already been won:

I still love you and want to be with you.

We are both responsible for the pains we have gone through.

Neither of us is perfect. We both bring deep-seated problems and faults to our relationship – many dating back to our childhoods. These are extremely hard to notice, change and account for. We will do our best, but if we can't manage certain steps, we would at least like to confess that – like everyone else on the planet – we are a little mad, and we're deeply sorry for this. It's the way we're all built. We know we've brought trouble into one another's lives. Once more, sorry.

We want things to go better between us because we profoundly care about one another, despite everything. We admire each other still.

For things to go better, we will both need to be modest and newly humble. We will need to let go of some very entrenched positions. We will, the two of us, have to give up on the pleasures of feeling in the right.

The work we'll do together won't be fast – and it will at points be rather painful. But we're committed to being curious about one another, to acknowledging errors – and to hearing uncomfortable truths. We'll try not to get cross – and when we do a bit nevertheless, we'll try to figure it out and go easy on one another.

We will never be perfect.

We want love to work for us. That it hasn't been too simple so far is no indication of anything other than that what we're trying to do is very hard indeed. We do truly love each other, at least sometimes. We want this to work.

Signed:

Signed:

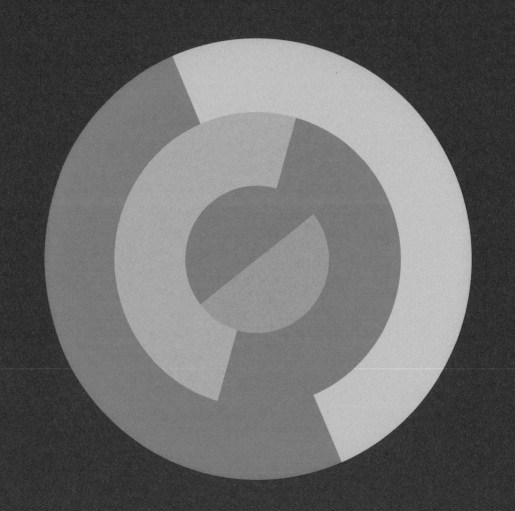

1.
The Scale of the Ambition

Part of the reason why relationships can often seem disappointing is that all of us probably have, somewhere in our unconscious, a memory of love having once been very much easier. Think of a newborn baby just after a feed. All its needs have, for now, been taken care of. A primordial bliss descends. It feels united with its parent, satiated, safe and utterly at peace.

Our idea of what a good, loving relationship should be like (and what it feels like to be loved) doesn't – it seems – ever just come from what we've experienced in adulthood; it arises from a stranger, more powerful source. The idea of happy coupledom taps into a fundamental picture of comfort, deep security, wordless communication and of our needs being effortlessly understood that comes from early childhood.

At the best moments of childhood (if things went reasonably well), a loving parent offered us extraordinary satisfaction. They knew when we were hungry or tired, even though we couldn't explain. We did not need to strive. They made us feel completely safe. We were held peacefully. We were entertained and indulged. And even if we don't recall the explicit details, the experience of being cherished has made a profound impression on us; it has planted itself in our deep minds as the ideal template of what love should be.

As adults, without really noticing, we continue to be in thrall to this notion of being loved, projecting the best experience of our early years into our present relationships and finding them sorely wanting as a result – a comparison that is profoundly corrosive and unfair.

So part of what we need to work on is our expectations. The love we received from a parent when we were a baby can't ever be a sound model for our later, adult experience of love. The reason is fundamental: We were relatively simple and tiny then, we are an adult now – a dichotomy with several key ramifications.

For a start, our needs were so much easier to fulfil. As babies, we needed to be washed, amused, put to bed. But we didn't need someone to trawl intelligently through the troubled corners of our minds. We didn't need a caregiver to understand why we prefer the first series of a television show to the second, why it is necessary to see our aunt on Sunday, or why it matters to us that the curtains harmonise with the sofa covers or that the bread must be cut with a proper bread knife. The parent knew absolutely what was required in relation to basic physical and emotional requirements. Our partner is stumbling in the dark around needs that are immensely subtle, far from obvious and very complicated to deliver on.

Secondly, none of it was reciprocal. The parent was intensely focused on caring for us, but they knew and totally accepted that we wouldn't engage with their needs. They didn't for a second imagine that they could take their troubles to us or expect us to nurture them. They didn't need us to ask them about their day. Our responsibility was blissfully simple: All we had to do to please them was to exist. Our most ordinary actions – rolling over on our tummy, grasping a biscuit in our tiny hand – enchanted them with ease. We were loved, we didn't have to love: a distinction between kinds of love which language normally artfully blurs, shielding us from the difference between being the privileged customer of love, or its more exhausted and long-suffering provider.

Furthermore, our parents were probably kind enough to shield us from the burden that looking after us imposed on them. They maintained a reasonably sunny façade until they retired to their own bedroom, at which point the true toll of their efforts could be witnessed (but by then we were asleep). They did us the honour of not quite showing us what looking after us cost them, which was immensely kind but did us one lasting disservice: It may unwittingly have created an expectation of what it would mean for someone to love us that was never true in the first place. We might in later life end up with lovers who are tetchy with us, who are too tired to talk at the end of the day, who don't marvel at our every antic, who can't even be bothered to listen to what we're saying – and we might feel (with some bitterness) that this is not how our parents were. The irony, which has its redeeming side, is that, in truth, this is exactly how our parents were, just up in their bedroom, when we were asleep and realised nothing.

The source of our present sorrow is not, therefore, a special failing on the part of our adult lovers. They are not tragically inept or uniquely selfish. It's rather that we're judging our adult experiences in the light of a very different kind of childhood love. We are sorrowful not because we have landed with the wrong person but because we have (sadly) been forced to grow up.

Let's begin this exercise by imagining what a baby (one to eight months old) needs from its parent to feel safe and happy. Let's try to make a list:

What a baby needs to be happy:		
FOOD	CARE	LAUGHTER
TOUCH	PATIENCE	CLOTHES
WARMTH	SENSORY	CUDDLES

We haven't given you much room, deliberately so. We think the box is going to be filled with a list that is as essential as it is limited (it may include milk, a cuddle, warmth in it …).

Then let's turn our minds to adults. What do we need from one another in order to be happy?

We all carry around in our heads a picture of what an ideal partner should do around us, how they should behave and what we want them to understand about us. We're asking for compatibility around such things as:

- who to see for dinner
- where to holiday
- what music to listen to
- what political party to support
- how to raise a child
- how much money to spend and on what
- how to decorate a home
- where to put dirty towels
- how to use a breadboard
- how much time to spend with our parents and theirs

- how we need to be supported when we're sad
- how we need to be engaged with when we're expansive and excited
- what to do about our jealousy
- how to handle our urge to stray
- what to do with the toilet seat
- when and how much to use our phones
- how to approach existential loneliness and dread

And that's just to start a list that could, in fairness, run to a volume, at least …

Make a start on your own lists by turning to the next page.

Sara ♡

Let's try to answer the following as ambitiously as possible:

What I need to be ideally happy with a partner.

When I'm tired, my partner should ...

....

In relation to sex, my partner should ...

....

Around holidays, my partner should ...

....

When it comes to their friends and family, my partner should ...

....

Around the house, my partner should ...

....

With money, my partner should ...

....

With the children, my partner should ...

....

When I've been unreasonable, my partner should ...

....

When I feel restless, my partner should ...

....

When I feel anxious, my partner should ...

....

Let's try to answer the following as ambitiously as possible:
What I need to be ideally happy with a partner.

When I'm tired, my partner should …

In relation to sex, my partner should …

Around holidays, my partner should …

When it comes to their friends and family, my partner should …

Around the house, my partner should …

With money, my partner should …

With the children, my partner should …

When I've been unreasonable, my partner should …

When I feel restless, my partner should …

When I feel anxious, my partner should …

The Scale of the Ambition

Some of the complexity and precision of our answers should make us laugh a little – in a dark way. It isn't that our desires are absurd, it's just that the possibility of them all being fulfilled by one person in this life must appear, in the cold light of day, rather remote.

Looking at the two lists side by side, it grows striking just how much we're hoping for from one another. We should consider how odd our lists would look from a historical perspective. For most of human history, no one expected to do more than tolerate their partner; all one wished for from a spouse was to find someone with whom to raise the next generation and maybe pool together a few farm implements. It's only in the last few minutes of our evolution as a species that we have come to expect to locate a partner who can be our ideal friend, sex partner, co parent, chauffeur, household manager and helpmate.

We deserve a significant dose of sympathy: We've entered the world of relationships at a very peculiar historical point, when being a couple is the focus of immense expectations and yet when we still have few implements and ideas with which to handle the rough patches – which means that there's now an almost infinite number of ways in which we can feel let down and at sea.

The odds are inevitably stacked against all our adult needs being seamlessly taken care of by any creature we're likely to cross paths with. This should make us not furious, but compassionately kind towards ourselves – and the flawed but in many ways good enough lovers we have already located.

2.
The Dangerous Quest for Compatibility

The modern understanding of love is dominated by a quest for compatibility.

Think back to your exes. In what ways were you not really compatible?

Communication
style
Morals
Goals
Raising kids
Finances
Spontaneous
Didn't meet needs
Lack of Jesus

Style (Lifestyle)
Morals
Raising kids
View of family
Emotionally unavailable
↳ didn't meet needs
Lack of depth
Lack of intimacy

Compatibility is not the precondition of love; it is the achievement of love.

Gustav Klimt, *The Kiss*, 1907–1908

The longing for compatibility had a sweet early expression in the writings of the philosopher Plato. He playfully conjectured that once in the long-distant past, all of us had actually been joined to someone else.

We were hermaphrodites, with four arms and legs and two faces stuck together pointing in different directions. But then the king of the gods, Zeus, grew jealous of human power and intelligence and, in a fit of rage, separated us all into individuals.

From that day on, said Plato, each of us has longed to refind the twin 'other half' from which Zeus's sword cruelly separated us.

That is what love is, in Plato's argument: the longing for (quite literally) the other half. Plato's idea is just a myth – but it tells us something about the longing we sometimes have when we search for love. We want to find someone who:

- will share our ideas on big things and small
- will agree with us when it counts
- will be very like us

We will – as it were – have found the missing twin.

Day to day, it's very easy to become aware of differences within couples, so it pays to take a step back and remember the degree to which, despite everything, you have been blessed with some serious areas of compatibility.

In what significant ways are you and your partner *compatible*?

lots of love to give	Morals/View Of Trinity
Willing to Communicate (learn)	Family Values
Goals / lifeStyle	Style - Lifestyle
Morals	Emotionally available
Raising a family	Willing to learn love/me
	N/A > Goals

What do you not argue about?

✱ We agree that we both argue about most things but feel its healthy & we leave nothing unresolved. ✱

But, of course, there is a darker side.

In what significant ways are you and your partner *incompatible*? N/A

✱ We don't agree w/ this.. ✱

What are the main topics you argue about?

- Communication	The way we communicate
- Reactions to conversation	How we can misunderstand the other
- Ways we were raised	Religions theology
- The bible / theology	The view of the World
' Viewing certain things	Driving (LoL)
different / opinions	

A big theme of this book is to alert both of you to the idea that we are collectively a little too concerned with the idea of finding compatibility. The search for it, though touching, is ultimately poisonous and deeply opposed to the true spirit of love.

The ideal partner for us is not someone who shares our every taste.

It is someone who knows how to negotiate differences in taste with sensitivity, insight and humour.

Compatibility is not the precondition of love; it is the achievement of love.

We need to accept that no partner can ever understand more than a percentage of who and what we are. A degree of frustration and loneliness is fundamental to human existence – and if we continue to think of being somewhat misunderstood as illegitimate, we'll never be able to sustain love.

If we refuse ever to feel (somewhat) lonely in a couple, there will be no option but to end up alone.

Let's go back to Plato and dismiss his charming but truly dangerous idea. We have no soulmate. There is no such thing as an 'other half'. We are all beautifully unusual individuals who have to work out how to accommodate our jagged, irregular characters.

3.
The True Romance of Pessimism

We're taught to think that a 'Romantic' attitude involves being extremely optimistic about how things might go with a partner. We're taught to think that hope is the oxygen of true love.

Far from it. A calculated dose of pessimism about how things might go is, in fact, the true friend of love – and the catalyst for tolerance and patience.

Pessimism is the ingredient we desperately need in order to dampen the wilder expectations that undermine our chances of making love work.

A pessimistic pledge:

No one can fully understand anyone else.

A degree of loneliness is the norm.

It isn't a sign your life has gone wrong.

It's conclusive proof it's going according to plan.

We want to introduce you to one of our favourite philosophers, Søren Kierkegaard.

This is one of our favourite quotes from his early work *Either/Or*, which we believe usefully fosters a pessimistic attitude:

> *Marry, and you will regret it; don't marry, you will also regret it; marry or don't marry, you will regret it either way. Laugh at the world's foolishness, you will regret it; weep over it, you will regret that too; laugh at the world's foolishness or weep over it, you will regret both. Believe a woman, you will regret it; believe her not, you will also regret it … Hang yourself, you will regret it; do not hang yourself, and you will regret that too; hang yourself or don't hang yourself, you'll regret it either way; whether you hang yourself or do not hang yourself, you will regret both. This, gentlemen, is the essence of all philosophy.*

Niels Christian Kierkegaard,
Unfinished sketch of Søren Kierkegaard, circa 1840

Now it is time for an exercise.

We are often obsessed with the idea that, in order for a relationship to work, our partner is going to have to change a lot and rather fast.

And yet the truth is that:

Other people rarely change – and when they do, change comes very slowly, and only when we push for it least.

Let's list what we find most irritating/frustrating/~~saddening~~ about our partner:

-
-
-
-
-
-
-
-
-

- Won't let me finish a sentence
- Differences in opinions
-
-
-
-
-

Now imagine that we might have to live with this list, that change wasn't going to be possible.

Could it still – despite everything – be bearable?

Don't answer immediately. But, in many cases, the answer might be a very quiet …

'yes'.

4.
Why on Earth Am I With *This* Person?

At the start of relationships, we often can't seem to thank the universe enough for bringing us together with an extraordinary being.

But after a while, we may curse the unusual bad luck we've suffered in tying up our lives with someone so distinctly frustrating and obtuse.

We need a helpful perspective drawn from psychotherapy. It was not quite an accident that we ended up together with this person. There are some deep-seated reasons, which we need to understand and make our peace with, as to why we are here and not with someone else. We don't have total freedom about who we get together with. The difficulties we're facing aren't coincidental bits of misfortune; they indicate the constraints of our respective psychologies.

At the heart of the modern idea of how we should find love is the notion that we must 'follow our instincts'. For most of human history, following our instincts was definitely not on the agenda; we followed the rational logic of those who set us up with partners for practical reasons. The modern, Romantic notion of love was born out of a radical, hopeful rejection of this cold logic.

The modern idea of love suggests that following our instincts is a reliable and wise way to identify a plausible candidate with whom to spend the next fifty years. Following our instincts may sound pleasant, but there is one large problem associated with this method: *Our instincts are – very often – deeply flawed, for reasons that take us back to childhood.*

When we look for partners, we're in important ways looking to *refind* emotions and styles of loving that we experienced when we were small, at the hands of our parents. This is sometimes very sweet and natural – but there's a whole set of problems associated with the repetition or rehearsal of themes from childhood. Parental figures may have not just loved us with understanding, tolerance and thoughtfulness. They may have mixed up their love with a host of problematic dynamics – dynamics that we now need to find present in any adult lover before we can experience ourselves as being 'in love' with them.

We may have once rejected certain candidates who were, on paper, attractive, competent and very loving – and we may not even have known

Hugues Merle, *Maternal Affection*, 1867

why we were rejecting them, while being compelled by other people. We might have come away from many dates saying of someone that they were 'a bit boring' or 'strangely unsexy'. But that's not really what we might have meant. What we really meant was that that person was *unlikely to make me suffer in the particular ways I require in order to experience myself as being 'in love'.*

The dark truth about love is often that we may not primarily want to be happy with the partner we choose. We want the partner to feel *familiar* – which may mean something very different from happiness.

Our not very satisfying partners seem like a mistake, but it's far more intentional than this. We may have little option but to follow a path of unhappy love that was laid down in childhood.

Try thinking about the difficult traits you're attracted to by completing the exercise on the next page.

Let's try an exercise:

Think back to the parent whose gender you're attracted to.

What are their most negative traits?:

Now, how many of these traits are present in your partner?

Let's try an exercise:
Think back to the parent whose gender you're attracted to.

What are their most negative traits?:

Now, how many of these traits are present in your partner?

Why on Earth Am I With *This* Person?

We call this need to refind problems from childhood in our adult love stories the Repetition Dynamic.

When friends and outsiders look at people in the grip of a troublesome Repetition Dynamic, they tend to say two things:

A. leave them
B. find someone easier, nicer, better … !

But we're very pessimistic about whether human beings can ever fully change the kinds of people they are attracted to. There were strong reasons why you picked who you picked. And that's OK.

So we have a different solution: We shouldn't try to change who we are attracted to. We should try to change the way we *characteristically deal with the difficulties that our types cause us.*

We seek out difficult lovers who mirror difficult parents or caregivers we knew in childhood. This tends to mean that *the way we are dealing with difficult characteristics in adulthood is the same as the way in which we learnt to deal with these characteristics in childhood.* We are probably responding rather childishly to the problems today's partner is throwing up.

We are dealing with the difficulties we are attracted to *in the manner of the children we once were.* Our pattern of response is riddled with some of the problems that a young person might make in relation to a difficult parent/caregiver.

Here are some child-like patterns of response to difficult lovers:

We over-personalise issues that we are not responsible for.	We get unproductively furious.
We assume we deserve punishment.	We sulk rather than explain.
We attention seek.	We withdraw.
	We panic.

It's very understandable and deeply forgivable that we might have learnt to respond in this way to difficult people. As children, we didn't have many options. We did what we could; we didn't have all the tools and all the right understanding. That said, there is an enormous opportunity to move ourselves from a child-like to an adult pattern of response in relation to the difficulties we are attracted to.

What may be truly making our relationships hard is not simply that we're attracted to tricky people (perhaps someone who is a bit fiery or distant or manically busy), it's also that we continue to react to tricky people now as we did then.

However, there is a properly grown-up – less agitated, less fragile – response that in principle we could adopt *and that would make all the difference.*

Consider this table, which tries to show how we might move from a child's reaction to a more ideal adult response.

A. Partner's tricky behaviour:	B. Child-like response on our part:	C. More adult response we should aim for:
Raising voice	'It's all my fault …'	'This is their issue: I don't have to feel bad.'
Patronising	'I'm stupid.'	'There are lots of kinds of intelligence. Mine is fine.'
Morose	'I have to fix you.'	'I'll do my best, but I'm not ultimately responsible for your mindset – and this doesn't have to impact on my self-esteem.'
Overbearing	'I deserve this.'	'I'm not intimidated by you.'
Distracted, preoccupied	Attention seeking: 'Notice me.'	'You're busy, I'm busy, that's OK …'

Our past may have assigned us an instinctive attraction towards people who can be challenging. But how we deal with them – once we're together – is open to revision. It makes all the difference if we can move from a child-like to a more adult response (column B to C).

Consider the child-like responses you might have used in the past, and think about a more ideal adult response by filling in the table on the next page.

Try filling in this table:

Think back to the difficult trait you're attracted to and list the possible child-like and adult responses to it.

Difficult trait I'm attracted to:	Child-like response to it:	Potentially more adult response to it:

Try filling in this table:
Think back to the difficult trait you're attracted to and list the possible child-like and adult responses to it.

Difficult trait I'm attracted to:	Child-like response to it:	Potentially more adult response to it:

Why on Earth Am I With *This* Person?

5.
What We Should Learn From One Another

A lot of what originally drew us to our partner was a desire for strengths that we don't ourselves possess.

Here are some typical examples of how our 'weaknesses' – by which we mean deficiencies, frailties, imperfections – can drive our search for a lover:

- We might be over-intellectual …
  and they are delightfully down to earth.
- We are a bit flighty and chaotic …
  and they are wonderfully ordered and precise.

My weaknesses:	The strengths that attract me:
Easily rattled	Calm, steadfastness
Conformist, rule-bound	Creativity, authenticity
Emotionally reserved, inhibited	Warmth, exuberance
Shy	Confidence
Chaotic	Order

Complete this exercise for yourselves.

My weaknesses:

The strengths that attract me:

We are often drawn to a partner because they have a quality we don't have. We want – in theory – to learn from that quality and absorb it into ourselves. And so we will be happy. That is the theory.

But to absorb the strengths of our partner, and thus become complete, two things must happen:

A. We need to be willing to *learn* things.
B. Our partner must be willing to *teach* us things.

And vice versa. The success of love is going to depend on success in learning and teaching.

The problem is, most of us are not very good at either of these.

First: we don't 'learn' from our partner's 'strengths'

In practice, we end up not learning from our partner's strengths, because learning can feel very humiliating. It means having to take on board that we're not as perfect as we think we are, that we need to make some perhaps quite big changes to the way we are now and how we do things.

When learning is a bore, we start to attack the 'teacher's' strengths that we'd originally been attracted to. We denigrate them because it would be so arduous to change. We suddenly and conveniently feel we're fine as we are.

We'd liked them for being down to earth, but now we call them simple-minded. We'd liked them for being ordered and precise, but now we call them anal and rigid.

Second: our partner doesn't 'teach' us very nicely how to absorb their 'strengths'

We may be bad students, but we are likely also – both of us – to be bad 'teachers'. We both know how to do things the other can't. But we tend to teach these things in a very counter-productive, impatient and stern way. We get irritated by our partner's incapacities and panicked by their frustrating natures. (The thought at the back of our minds is often: 'I'm together with a fool. They must understand now!' We don't have a good teacher's confidence in gradual progress.)

We can see they're not very creative – but rather than gently coax them towards greater creativity, we lose our tempers and call them 'sterile'. Or we can see that they're not good at practical things – but rather than gently coax them towards greater competence, we lose our tempers and call them 'a childish mess'. So what had started as a beautiful promise of completion ends up as warfare, with both parties not actually completing each other, but instead resenting and denigrating their respective strengths while not nurturing and healing their respective weaknesses.

Let's see how that unfortunate cycle might look on a chart:

Our weaknesses:	Strengths that attract us:	How we denigrate these strengths:
Too rigid, ordered	Creativity, imagination	'Dreamer, fantasist, lazy'
Too messy, chaotic	Discipline, competence	'Cold, frigid, anal'

We all do this; it's a sad cycle:

We said we wanted someone:	What we end up feeling about them/calling them:
Laid-back	Lazy
Calm	Inert
Practically minded	Trivial
Imaginative	Dreamer
Warm	Stifling

Here is a lesson plan for the future. Discuss the following:

What are your distinct areas of competence (emotional and practical)?

When you haven't in the past taught your partner very calmly about them, what did you do?

How might you proceed differently in the future?

6.
The Secret Lives of Other Couples

A question that rarely leaves us alone in love is: What exactly are other people's relationships like?

This is far from a piece of disinterested sociological curiosity. What we urgently seek to know is: Are other people in as much trouble as we are? After a furious row over nothing very much at eleven at night, or after yet another month that has unfolded with almost no sex, we wonder how statistically normal our case might be – precisely because it threatens to feel like a unique curse.

Most of us have a handful of relationships – maybe four or five – that we know and keep in mind as standards of what we understand by normality. Perhaps we met these couples at university or they live on our street and are at a comparable stage of life. Without knowing they are playing this role, these sample couples function for us as our secret spirit level of love.

At tennis, we notice how kind they are to one another, as well as how energetic and lithe they remain. Over dinner, we note how much respect they show to one another's opinions. In the taxi on the way home, we spot the tender way they hold each other's hands. And, naturally, we feel both highly abnormal and very wretched as a result.

But our assessment of our love stories suffers from a basic and unfair asymmetry: We know our own relationships from the inside but generally only encounter the relationships of others in heavily edited and sanitised form from the outside. We see other couples chiefly in social situations where politeness and cheeriness are the rule. We trust their blithe summaries of their lives. But we don't have access to footage from the bedroom, the uncut transcriptions of their rows or their raw night-time streams of consciousness.

However, we have all this and more about ourselves. We can't help but be intently aware of our own relationship's sorrows and absurdities: the cold silences, harsh criticisms, furious outbursts, episodes of door slamming, bitter late-night denunciations, simmering sexual disappointments and times of aching loneliness in the bedroom.

Because of this asymmetry, quite understandably, we come to the conclusion that our own relationships are a great deal darker and far more painful than is common. In times of distress, we fling a definitive accusation at our partner: 'No one else has to put up with this.'

We need, to be fairer on ourselves and our beloved, to create space in our minds for the scale of our ignorance. We simply don't know. We are lacking data. We owe ourselves a richer picture of love than we have yet secured. This isn't prying or cruel, we just need to better understand the true nature of the task we're undertaking.

The truth is that misery – or at least some kinds of very serious longing and scratchiness – is the rule, far more than public sources will ever admit. It's not that we as a couple are strangely awful or damned, it's that relationships themselves are an essentially and inescapably difficult project.

Part of the reason we get it so wrong is that we have the wrong kind of art: the movies we watch are oddly coy, the novels don't tell it how it is. It's a mark of the problem that we almost never leave a cinema or close a novel thinking: that's just like my life.

The dominant emotion in most relationships is ambivalence; that is, a complex mixture of love *and* hatred, contentment *and* confinement, loyalty *and* betrayal. Most loves are too good to leave, yet too compromised to generate profound contentment. They subsist in a grey zone, where moments of joy bleed into stretches of melancholy, where at points we sob and are certain our partner has ruined our lives and then, the following morning, assisted by sunshine and a brisk coffee, we recover a feeling that things are basically fine.

If we could properly see – via tenderly accurate films and novels and chats in group therapy or with older honest couples – the reality of pretty much any relationship, we might arrive at a surprising and deeply heartening conclusion: that our own relationship is, in fact, two things above all – very normal and good enough.

To help us get a more accurate picture of what all couples go through, we've made a wide survey of the complaints that couples from around The School of Life community have made about one another.

What percentage of these people do you think reported the following problems? (See below for the answers.)

My partner:

1. is difficult around sex (preoccupied by fantasies, loses interest, not spontaneous, etc.)

2. isn't warm enough

3. is too cold and distant

4. doesn't listen properly

5. has reacted very badly when I've made a reasonable complaint

6. can be very stubborn

7. acts at times as if they don't even like me

8. has put me down in front of other people

9. dislikes my wardrobe choices on a semi-regular basis, even if they don't say it explicitly

10. makes arguments worse by insulting me

11. misunderstands me in important ways

12. is willing to take other people's side against me

13. regularly refuses to see my point of view

14. continues to do something that upsets me, after I've pointed it out

15. gets very moody

In another research exercise at The School of Life, we sought out four established couples – selected because they came across as charming, pleasant and comfortable with each other – and we invited them to reveal some of their most intimate grievances.

What they said about each other suggests that feeling one's partner is, in specific areas, really awful is a standard, ordinary, almost inevitable consequence of being in a long-lasting relationship. The results of the survey can be seen on the next page.

Answers:
All 100 percent, except 1 – ninety-four percent; 8 – eighty-three percent; 10 – ninety-four percent.

My partner always leaves their dirty clothes on the floor.

My partner spends a lot more money than me. They are always buying things they don't really need.

They police my diet, always urging me to eat more broccoli, etc. Once when I bought some chocolate they threw it in the bin; they go on about my zinc levels.

They sigh in this ridiculous way when they're pretending they're hard done by; it's so pathetic it makes me want to scream.

They're so envious – and in a mean way: If someone's successful, they are always snide and can't wait to find something to criticise them for.

At dinner parties my partner will often cut across me when I'm saying something – they say I'm not telling a story the right way, I'm boring everyone, I'm being too heavy and serious. It's humiliating.

Around advice my partner has blind trust in anything anyone says. If the plumber says it's going to take six months to fix the boiler, that must be true; they never think there's any need to get a second opinion. They just never listen to me!

My partner snores in bed – really loudly.

If I do something obviously nice for them, my partner gets suspicious: 'What are you being nice for?' It's so perverse it drives me nuts.

They always pick the worst moments to mention annoying issues: We could be gazing at the ocean and they'd go, 'You know, in twenty years time there won't be any butterflies in Norway.' Just give me five minutes away from the troubles of the world.

My partner has got these incredibly precise sexual fixations – particular clothes, specific words (and how I need to say them), special ways of touching them. If I don't do it exactly right, they get really upset.

They're so clumsy; they're always spilling things in the kitchen, cutting their fingers. At the airport I know they're going to trundle their suitcase into someone.

When I'm in the middle of saying something, they'll suddenly ask a random question about something totally unrelated.

They leave hairs in the bathroom basin. I've mentioned it about fifty times but now I've given up – they just say it doesn't matter. I can't tell anyone because they'd think I was an idiot to live with someone so disgusting.

They spilled wine over an antique rug – by mistake, but they didn't try not to. It's as if they've got this strategy to make sure the house can't be the way I want it to be.

Their political opinions have become embarrassing. I'm constantly on edge when we're with friends in case they start coming out with their ridiculous attitudes.

7.
Continuing the Conversation

One of the most dispiriting things about living around someone for a long time is that we end up assuming that we know them rather well – and, therefore, we get bored when we shouldn't. We believe that we know almost every one of their anecdotes; we think we can finish all of their sentences. We assume that they could not surprise us any more.

And yet an astonishing truth deserves our full recognition: *We continue not to know them at all.* We may spend a few decades around someone and, if things go as they usually do, grasp only a sliver of them. It is just that we have stopped talking to them properly, as we did in the early days. We mistake familiarity with knowledge; we confuse having them around with grasping their identity.

Our curiosity falls victim to a structural arrogance. We end up chatting over the day-to-day and miss out the vast, poignant themes that play themselves out in the other's life.

Paradoxically, the longer we are together, instead of becoming more nuanced and complete, our picture of our partner can get reduced and distorted. We grow so focused on what's happening in the practical realm that we lose sight of the way thousands of experiences – still unknown to us – have shaped who our partner is. We stop chatting about their past, which is what we often need to understand to arrive at a more generous and forgiving view of their present behaviour. And we cease to enquire about their ever-changing view of their own future and aspirations.

A conversation *ritual* sounds odd because we imagine that good conversations should be spontaneous, lucky accidents. Yet to call for a conversation ritual involves accepting the pessimistic truth that the ordinary pressures and habits of life will get in the way of prolonged, exploratory, mutual encounters – and that we'll need to take specific measures to get ourselves back into a proper inquisitive mode.

Set aside regular time to ask each other some of the following:

Aspirations

What do you still want to achieve in life?

What motivates you?

Describe a typical day in our lives together ten years from now ...

I'd love you not to laugh if I tell you that one of my secret aspirations is ...

What makes you particularly happy?

What values do you think we share?

What could still be fun?

The Past

What was especially hard for you when you were little?

What are the good things you learnt from your mother? And your father?

What are the bad things you learnt from your mother? And your father?

How have you changed over the past few years?

In what ways are we trying, in our present, to change the patterns of the past?

Describe a typical weekend when you were about ten.

Describe yourself at around twenty.

Continuing the Conversation

Forgiveness

Which of your flaws would you like to be forgiven for?

How have I let you down?

What are you sad about?

How could I do better?

What I never get around to telling you often enough is …

I recognise I might be quite hard to live with because …

What two habits of mine would you love me to change?

And what two bad habits of mine could you learn to live with?

If you never improved one bit, I …

In the midst of the most bitter fight, please always remember that …

Tastes

What books do you now enjoy reading?

Describe an ideal holiday.

What moves you in a film?

How do you think your tastes in food are changing?

What are your political views? How are they evolving?

How would you define your philosophy of life?

What have you learnt since New Year?

8.
Overcoming Our Parents

There is a move many of us make in the heat of an argument with our partner that is at once devastating, accurate and entirely uncalled for. In a particularly contemptuous, sly and yet gleeful tone, partners are inclined to announce, as if a rare truth was being unearthed: *You're turning into your mother/father.*

The claim is apt to silence us because, however much we may have tried to develop our own independent characters, we can't help but harbour a deep and secret fear that we are prey to an unconscious psychological destiny. In one side of our brains, we are aware of a range of negative qualities we observed in our parents that we sense are intermittently hinted at in our own personalities. And we are terrified.

We catch ourselves rehearsing opinions that once struck us as patently absurd or laughable. In moments of weakness, we find ourselves replaying just the same sarcastic or petty, vain or angry attitudes we once felt sure we would never want to emulate. The accusations of our partner hurt so much because they knock up against a genuine risk.

At the same time, the criticism is deeply underhand. Firstly, because even if we ourselves occasionally share an account of our parents' failings with our partner, the universal rules of filial loyalty mean that we – and only we – are ever allowed to bring these up again in an aggressive tone.

Secondly, the accusation is unfair because it is attempting to push us into denying something that is invariably partly correct. How could we not be a little like our parents, given the many years we spent around them, the untold genes we share with them and the malleability of the infant mind?

We should never get railroaded into protesting that we are unlike those who put us on the earth; we should undercut the implicit charge by immediately candidly admitting that we are – of course – very much like our parents, as our partner is akin to theirs. How could we be anything else? Why wouldn't we be? But, in a twist to the normal argument, we should then remind our partner that we chose to be with them precisely in order to attenuate the risks of an unexamined parental destiny. It was and remains their solemn duty not to mock us for being like our parents, but to assist us with kindness to become a little less like them where it counts.

By hectoring and accusing us, they aren't identifying a rare truth from which we hide away in shame; they are stating the obvious and then betraying the fundamental contract of adult love. Their task as our partner isn't to bully us into making confessions that we would have been ready to accept from the start; it's to help us to evolve away from the worst sides of people who have inevitably messed us up a little and yet whom we can't (of course, despite everything) stop loving inordinately.

Let's start positively:
What positive traits did you inherit from your father?

What positive traits did you inherit from your mother?

Now for the more delicate part:

What negative traits did you inherit from your father?

What negative traits did you inherit from your mother?

But there is redemption available too:
How would you like to outstrip your father emotionally?

How would you like to outstrip your mother emotionally?

This is the key bit:
How could I help you to evolve beyond your parents?

9

A Trust Check-Up

It's natural to assume that we trust our partner intuitively and generously. After all, we may have built a complex life together; we may have children with them, a joint mortgage and plans to hand them everything we own in our will. Surely, of all people in the world, it should be them we can trust …

But matters are never quite so simple. It might be that we repeatedly suspect that our partner, however much we want to love them and believe in their good faith, is someone who we believe might be about to harm, belittle or forget about us. This might be true or, more poignantly, essentially a spectre in our heads …

Confusingly, we're not usually very good at seeing in detail how much (or how little) we trust our partner – or at accurately grasping their level of trust in us. Suppose a stranger grabs our suitcase off the carousel at the airport – do we instantly think they are a thief or do we assume that they must have made an innocent mistake? The difference lies in the picture we develop of the motives at play. The mark of the trusting person at the carousel isn't that they can't imagine anyone taking their bag, but that they always first calmly assume that it's extremely unlikely that anyone would take their bag other than by accident. They are slow to panic.

Similarly, in a relationship, the trusting partner isn't beyond thinking that their companion might hurt them; it's just that their operating assumption is always for a long time that the partner is on their side.

Yet this kind of trust is an emotional luxury that some of us have simply not grown up with or been able to acquire through positive past relationships. For the trust-poor in love, a standard view will be that, whatever kind words were said yesterday or at the altar, there is always going to be a danger that the partner could suddenly turn around and be very nasty or cruel. It can make us very hard to live around – especially when this isn't exactly true.

Because so many fights come down to issues of trust, it can help – in quiet moments – to audit our levels of this emotion and to recognise ourselves as, sometimes, being deficient in this area. We deserve not condemnation but extra degrees of love – as well as enormous rewards for having the courage to admit that there might be a problem with us here.

Consider the following statements and individually give each one a score from one to five, depending on the degree to which it reflects your feelings, with one being 'not very much' and five being 'very much indeed.'

Trust question: Score:

You are generally interested in what I think and feel, even if you don't always get round to showing your interest.

Despite my failings, you are basically on my side.

You've got our joint economic security in view.

When you criticise me, you have my interests at heart.

If I sincerely apologise, you'll start to forgive me.

If you promise to do something, you'll genuinely try to do it, even if things don't quite work out.

If I can find a way of explaining myself calmly, you'll at least understand my point of view, even if you don't agree with me.

You find me sexually attractive, even if there are lots of obstacles to having sex.

When you do things that I find humiliating, I realise you don't deliberately set out to hurt me.

Although there are others who have a claim on you, I can ultimately rely on you to put my needs above theirs.

When you're angry with me, there's still a lot of goodwill below the surface.

Total score:

Consider the following statements and individually give each one a score from one to five, depending on the degree to which it reflects your feelings, with one being 'not very much' and five being 'very much indeed.'

Trust question: **Score:**

You are generally interested in what I think and feel, even if you don't always get round to showing your interest.

Despite my failings, you are basically on my side.

You've got our joint economic security in view.

When you criticise me, you have my interests at heart.

If I sincerely apologise, you'll start to forgive me.

If you promise to do something, you'll genuinely try to do it, even if things don't quite work out.

If I can find a way of explaining myself calmly, you'll at least understand my point of view, even if you don't agree with me.

You find me sexually attractive, even if there are lots of obstacles to having sex.

When you do things that I find humiliating, I realise you don't deliberately set out to hurt me.

Although there are others who have a claim on you, I can ultimately rely on you to put my needs above theirs.

When you're angry with me, there's still a lot of goodwill below the surface.

Total score:

A Trust Check-Up

53

Add up your scores for the previous exercise. A score of forty-five or above indicates a very high general level of trust; a score of thirty or below suggests a challenging or low level.

Crucially, not being particularly trusting of your partner doesn't mean they must be untrustworthy; it could be that, for all kinds of understandable reasons, you have difficulty feeling trust even where it is merited.

Topics of conversation:
- What might have made trust difficult for you?
- Who was untrustworthy in your childhood?

Trust builds in three main ways:
A. When we get a more accurate understanding of our partner's motives and intentions – which generally turn out to be less negative than, in our anxiety, we had imagined.
B. When we understand what made trust hard for us in our past and realise that the way we were treated by certain people long ago doesn't have to determine how we will be treated by new people or our partner in the present.
C. When we ourselves become less fragile; that is, when we don't require so much reassurance, or such overt signalling, to feel relatively confident of our partner's goodwill. We don't lose belief in love just because it's not strongly on show for a while.

10.
How We See Ourselves –
And How Our Partner Sees Us

There is always a risk of a gap appearing between how we see ourselves and how our partner may see us.

We tend to assume that it is obvious to the other person that we are, essentially, quite good people; not always perfect, but on the right side of the line.

Yet how clearly does our self-conception tally with the reality as it seems through our partner's eyes?

We would be wise to check in occasionally …

This exercise has two rounds, one for each partner. In the first round, pick out some adjectives from the long list to indicate the way you see yourself. Pick out the seven most notable ones and write them in your 'how I see myself' column. They won't apply perfectly, because we're such complex creatures: We might be (for instance) adventurous in some areas of life but rather cautious in others. It doesn't need to be a word that suits you in every possible respect, but just one that has some resonance for you.

Then ask your partner to look at the list of adjectives and to pick out seven that seem to capture who they think you are (they don't have to be positive!). These should go in the 'how you see me' column.

Then repeat the exercise the other way, for the other partner.

A

abrasive, adventurous, agitated, ambitious, angry, anxious, arrogant, argumentative, assertive, awkward

B

boastful, bookish, bossy

C

calculating, calm, carefree, careful, careless, cautious, changeable, clever, clingy, clumsy, cold, competent, competitive, over-competitive, a complainer, complex, confident, confused, considerate, contrarian, conventional, creative, critical

D

dedicated, deep, defensive, demanding, devious, difficult, dignified, direct, disorganised, distant, domineering, dreamy, badly dressed, well dressed, driven

E

eccentric, eager, over-eager, elegant, eloquent, easily embarrassed, empathic, energetic, excitable

F

fashion-conscious, flexible, focused, forgetful, forgiving, formal, funny, fussy

G

generous, gentle, gloomy, a gossip, greedy, gregarious

H

hard to please, harsh, homely, humorous, hypocritical

I

imaginative, impulsive, inconsistent, indecisive, independent, individualistic, inflexible, insightful, intellectual, over-intellectual, intrusive, inward, ironic

J

jaded, judgemental

K

kindly

L

lazy, easily led, lonely, loud, loyal

M

manipulative, materialistic, melancholy, messy, modest, moody, motivated

N

nagging, naïve, natural, neat, needy, negative, neglectful, negligent, nervous, noisy, nosey

O

open, organised, outspoken, over-optimistic, overwhelmed

P

passionate, persuasive, playful, polite, practical, preoccupied, proud, prudish, puritanical

Q

quiet

R

realistic, refined, relaxed, reliable, reluctant, resentful, reserved, resilient, resourceful, rigid, rigorous, rude

S

sceptical, secretive, selective, self-centred, self-contained, self-critical, self-reliant, sensitive, sentimental, sensuous, serious, sexy, a show-off, shrewd, shy, silent, sly, snide, snobbish, soft, solemn, sophisticated, stand-offish, strategic, stressed, stubborn, sulky, suspicious, sympathetic

T

talkative, tasteful, teasing, tenacious, thin-skinned, thoughtful, timid, tired

U

unambitious, undignified, easily upset, unrealistic, unreasonable, unreliable, unshockable

V

vulgar, vulnerable

W

warm, wasteful, weak, weird, wild, wily, withholding, witty, worldly, a workaholic, a worrier

How I see myself:	How you see me:
1.	1.
2.	2.
3.	3.
4.	4.
5.	5.
6.	6.
7.	7.

Once the exercise is done, look at the discrepancies that crop up in each table. Talk them through in a kindly way.

How I see myself:	How you see me:
1.	1.
2.	2.
3.	3.
4.	4.
5.	5.
6.	6.
7.	7.

Conversation starters:

What might explain some of the discrepancies?

What led you to pick a few of the negative adjectives for your partner? What incidents come to mind?

How might we do better at explaining ourselves to one another?

Practise giving an explanation for a negative adjective (for you and your partner) that avoids blame and instead seeks to locate the most sympathetic explanation.

What bits of the other person's past might be invited to shed light on their negative adjectives?

What bits of your past might be used to shed a more forgiving light on your negative adjectives?

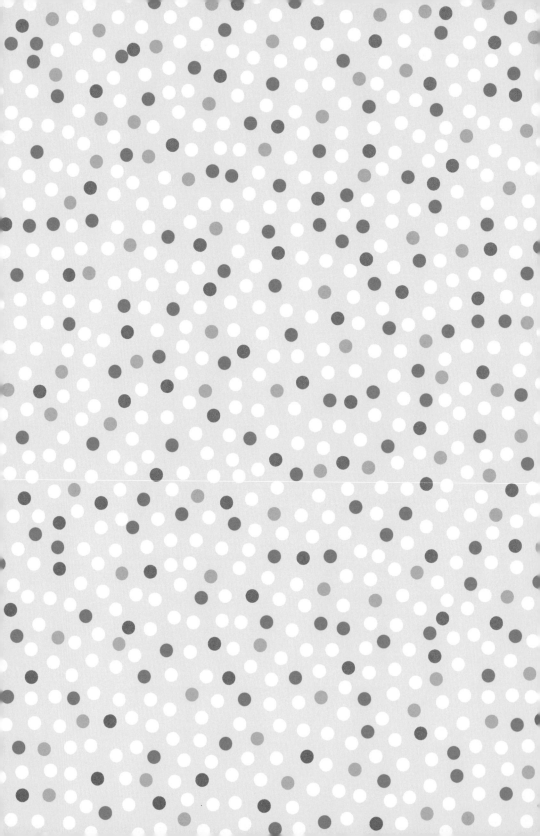

11.
The Little Things

Part one: Little things that get to us
There are lots of little things that our partner does that annoy us. It might be their habit of biting their lip, or the way they stick their elbow out when brushing their teeth, or the way they emphasise the word 'actually'; perhaps they leave doors slightly open, or maybe they hum quietly to themselves in the shower.

Stated plainly, these sound like extremely unimportant details. We know these might not bother other people at all; it's almost embarrassing to admit how much they upset us.

It's a problem not only because we're annoyed but also because our partner picks up on our irritation and feels – understandably – that it's deeply unfair: They accuse us of making a ridiculous fuss about nothing.

Normally, our instinct is to feel that we should try, if we possibly can, to put these things out of our mind, but a more productive approach is to take them very seriously and investigate them deeply. The small, annoying quirk can be treated as a symbol: It might look minor but it stands for something major. Just as a little row of small stars on the shoulder pads of a military uniform might look, to an outsider, like an irrelevant decorative flourish but to insiders they mean something huge, it's what they stand for that's significant.

Turn the page and, without thinking about it too much, each make a quick list of things your partner does that annoy you, irrespective of how trivial or bizarre they sound.

Part 1:

Make a list of all the little things your partner does that annoy you.

Little things that get to me: Analysis:

Part 1:
Make a list of all the little things your partner does that annoy you.

Little things that get to me:

Analysis:

The Little Things

Typically our irritation occurs so rapidly that we don't pause to spell out why these things get to us so much. We should – perhaps for the first time – decode every annoying symbolic detail and explain to ourselves, and to our partner, what it means to us. For instance:

Lip biting
When my partner bites their lip I feel they're secretly thinking of something quite important and then not saying it (my mother sometimes does this too). It bothers me because I know they've got something difficult on their mind but I don't know what it is. I fear my partner won't tell me about things that matter to them.

The lifted elbow while brushing their teeth
To me this action feels like they are taking up too much space, like they're trying to shove some imaginary person (who could be me) out of the way.

The word 'actually'
They say 'actually', and it feels to me as if they are laying claim to reality, that they know what's actual and, by implication, I don't. I'm being cast as dreamy and out of touch, which I don't think I am.

The slightly open door
For me a slightly open door means thoughtlessness, not picking up on a detail – nearly closed, properly closed, what's the difference? It's the attitude of a person who doesn't notice if you're upset or have bought a new pair of trousers or are feeling worried; they've got no feel for nuance.

The quiet humming
I think this is about being ignored – the humming is quiet, it's just for them, not for me; they're keeping this satisfied, contented part of themselves to themselves.

Return to the table on page 62. In the second column, explain as much as you can why particular details get to you: What do they mean, what do they symbolise, in your mind?

Curiously, the more we can get at the real, underlying issue, the less important the outward detail tends to feel.

Part two: little things that are nice

Even when there's a fair bit of conflict, there are still little things our partner does that strike us as sweet; there are moments when it's extremely nice being together. Perhaps they sent our mother a thoughtfully chosen birthday card or made a lovely tomato salad; maybe we like how they've arranged their desk, or at one point when they're saying something they shrug their shoulders in a charming way; or maybe we're touched by how devotedly they do their stretching exercises every morning.

On the table on page 68, quickly note down a handful of modest things, however slight, about your partner that you find rather appealing or endearing.

Although we like these things, they can feel pretty minor when set beside the bigger problem areas, so they don't carry very much weight in our overall view of our partner. We notice them for a moment, then they get swamped by everything else that's going on.

But if we examine the small pleasures of being together more carefully, it often turns out that they're indicating a bigger and deeper idea: We're getting a glimpse of something important about our relationship. For instance:

The birthday card to my mother
Underlying goodwill. You being nice to her is a way of being loyal to me. I know you're not a natural fit with her; you're being diplomatic and generous – qualities I sometimes forget you have.

The tomato salad
It's a very simple thing but I really like it. It signals a quality in you; you can home in on essentials and make them work well. You're unpretentiously stylish.

The way your desk is arranged
Neat but not fussy, organised without being oppressive or cold.

The charming shrug
Suggests humorous irony; a kind of 'isn't that so ridiculous' gesture that's quite warm and generous, implying 'but then we're all pretty ridiculous aren't we, especially me'.

The stretching exercises

A sense of you being really willing to make an effort, even though it's not that much fun at the time. It's nothing to do with vanity, it's a sign of your touchingly dutiful side.

In the second column of the table on page 68, expand as much as you can on why this little thing appeals to you: What is it about it that speaks to you; what is it saying about your partner at the deepest level?

Seeing each other's lists and explanations reverses the normal trend of life. We tend to hear so much more about what our partner is upset by than what they find charming. And precisely because these are seemingly minor details, they are exactly the sorts of things that don't get commented on in our ordinary days and nights. We're starting to rebalance our sense of how we see each other.

Part 2:

Make a list of all the little things your partner does that you find endearing.

Nice little things about you: Analysis:

Part 2:

Make a list of all the little things your partner does that you find endearing.

Nice little things about you:

Analysis:

The Little Things

12.
How We Like to Be Loved

One of the key desires of love is the wish to help another person. But an intention doesn't always or automatically translate into a ready capacity for true assistance.

Picture a five-year-old who has stumbled into his parents' bedroom and surprised his mother crying. She is normally so strong and ready with help for him. Now he longs to do something to staunch the tears, but he is at sea (the sobs might be about the mortgage, a turbulent time at work or an argument with her partner – but all these aren't for a child to grasp). He sweetly suggests a glass of water – and pipes up that he might run downstairs to get Knitted Rabbit.

The impulse to help floats logically free of any actual ability to do so. Two people can long to be supportive and generous to one another and yet lack all the skills to deliver on their good intentions – and therefore end up feeling isolated, resentful and unloved.

We cause ourselves trouble because we are too slow to recognise an odd, largely unmentioned phenomenon: how varied and particular our notions of help can be. We take our own preferred style of being soothed as the natural starting point for how to soothe others – but when we are wrong, and our partner's original distress is compounded by their sense of having been ignored or insulted, we take them to be ungrateful and cruel, and vow never to attempt to be kind again.

An urgent task is therefore to try to understand the particular way in which we, and our partner, need love to be delivered in order to feel that it is real.

I. *Listening*

We might be the type who, when sad or in difficulty, needs first and foremost to speak. What we say may not be entirely sequential. We might go back over things a few times and omit to cap our stories with neat endings. But that might not matter, because what we want above all from a partner when we are suffering is that they sit with us at length and listen. We want them to signal their engagement with their eyes but not their mouths, to register our anger, to observe our disappointment and, at most, to prompt us at opportune moments with a 'Go on' or a small supportive sound.

Yet what we absolutely don't want are answers, solutions or analyses, for them to open their wallets, to give us a plan or to rush to fill in our silences. We want them to sit listening because the real problem we need assistance with isn't so much the specific issue we are mentioning (the parking ticket, the in-laws, the delayed delivery), it's the overarching sense that most people we encounter can't really be bothered to take the time to imagine themselves correctly into our lives. Perhaps there was a history to this: our parents might have been practically minded, busy and successful but somehow rather callous and distracted in the way they sought always and immediately to push our difficulties out of the way with logic. Now we feel that an immediate 'solution' can be an excuse for not listening to the problem. That's why just being heard feels like the quintessence of love. We might almost deliberately take our time, go back over points our partner had thought were finished and re-explore a jagged bit of our story, not to mislead but because such rehearsals create the backdrop for the only style of help we crave and trust: receptive, quiet attention.

ii. Solutions

Then again, at another end of the spectrum, love might not feel real unless it is accompanied by precise and concrete solutions. Vague sympathy is worthless. We might want to hear a flow of ideas as to what we should do next, what sort of strategy we should deploy, whom we might call and how we can get answers. It's very well for someone to say they feel our pain, but we would prefer a plan. Love is a sheet of paper with a list of bullet points in your partner's handwriting.

In addition, we might not be averse to evidence that our partner has spent some money on our problems. Time isn't a currency we respect. We might want them to pay for an accountant or a lawyer – or offer an evening in an expensive restaurant. After an economically fragile childhood, to feel really helped, we might long for evidence of financial outlay. We can't be reassured just by what someone says; we have built up a residual suspicion and distrust around lone verbal offerings. We remember how nice it was when an elderly relative unexpectedly gave us a very well-chosen present when we were nine and in hospital after a bad fall. They never said very much to us (perhaps they were rather shy), but this gesture truly touched us. We felt sure of their kindness – as if for the first time – when we learnt just how much the present had cost.

iii. Optimism

Differently again, when we divulge our agonies, our priority may just be to hear that everything will eventually be OK. We don't mind a little exaggeration. Despair strikes us as cheap; reasons to give up are always obvious. For us, love is a species of hope.

IV. *Pessimism*

Or, alternatively, it's hope that may be enraging. What calms us down is a quiet walk around the prospect of catastrophe. We don't want to be alone in our fears. We long for someone to explore the grimmest possibilities with bleak sangfroid: to mention prison, insolvency, front-page headlines and the grave … Only when our partner is ready to match our most forbidding analyses can we be reassured we're in the hands not of a callous sentimentalist, but rather someone honest enough to see the dangers and to worry about them as much as we do – and perhaps to stick with us while we serve out the prison sentence.

V. *Cuddles*

A cuddle can sound to some like a petty response to bad news, but for us it can be the most reliable evidence of heartfelt love. To help our minds, we need someone first to reassure our bodies, to hold us tightly and quietly while we close our eyes in pain and surrender to their firm embrace. Help in adulthood may, for others, be associated with the gift of insight, but for us it is touch that soothes. We are picking up on memories of early childhood. Our wise parents knew that a distressed child does not need a lesson or a lecture; they should be laid down on the bed, held and have their head stroked by a soft, giant adult hand.

The misfortune lies in how easily we can irritate with the wrong offer of love – and in turn, how quickly we may be offended when our efforts go unappreciated. A gift of pessimism or optimism, of a cuddle or some cash, won't seem to the partner like a touchingly off-target act of kindness; it is likely to be read as an insulting failure to understand who they really are.

Recognising that there are different styles of help at least alerts us to the severe risks of misunderstanding. Instead of getting annoyed at our lover's inept (and sometimes widely misdirected) effort, we can grasp – perhaps for the first time – the basic truth that these blundering companions are in fact attempting to be nice. In turn, the clearest clue of the kind of help our partner wants is the help they offer us.

It seems love can't remain at the level of intentions alone. It must involve constant strenuous efforts to translate our wishes into interventions truly aligned with the psychology and history of another human being.

Discuss the following:
How do you like to be loved?

1. being listened to

2. being offered solutions

3. being offered optimistic prognoses

4. being offered pessimistic prognoses

5. being offered cuddles

What are the differences between you?

Let's think also of the past. Our styles of feeling loved owe a lot to childhood. For many years – as our minds were being formed – we were in powerful, intensely emotional relationships with people who cared for us. How we experienced love as a child will have a deep impact on our adult sense of what love is like.

Discuss the following:

What did your care givers do to make you feel loved as a child?

What were your parents' 'love signals', details of parental behaviour that made you feel cherished and appreciated?

These ideas might be deeply familiar to us – though, day to day, they are not necessarily at the front of our minds. We might never have explained them to our partner, stripping us of a vital chance to get our love across.

Across various areas, we should individually identify particularly resonant moments and experiences, such as:

- I would watch TV on the sofa with my grandparents.
- My father used to occasionally put his head on one side when he was really listening; he was thinking very hard about what I was saying.
- My mother would smile at me – not for any reason, just because she was happy I was me.
- When I was feeling upset, my mother used to make a very special sympathetic noise – not an actual word, more a sort of extended 'Ohh'; for me that sound means 'I love you'.
- I loved it when my mother stroked my hair.
- When my mother used to tuck me in at night, she'd partly remake the bed once I was in it; I felt like a little snail in my shell.
- One time, when I got home from school – probably I was about ten – I was really starving and my dad cooked a huge meal (it was lamb chops); he just kept offering me more and more and I kept saying, 'Yes, please'.

On the table overleaf, each draw up your own list of love signals from early life. Then discuss the following together:

What sorts of things are still love signals for you today?

What might your partner do to tap into them?

What might you do for them?

List the love signals from your early life.

List the love signals from your early life.

13.
Early Wounds

Part one: what happened?

Necessarily, there were things that went wrong in childhood: Our parents were imperfect; there were difficult situations we were exposed to; there were problems we had to face that we couldn't properly cope with at a young age. We've tried as best we can to adapt, but often these early wounds continue to exert a dark pressure deep into adult life. It can feel awkward to mention them because it can sound like we're just making excuses – but actually we're circling important facts about why we are the way we are. It can make a huge difference to our understanding of ourselves – and of our partner – to see where a problem might be coming from.

The first stage is to lay out what was difficult for us. We're trying to remember, in a detailed way, occasions on which we got very distressed or emotionally hurt. We're not trying to see them through our current adult eyes but to reconnect with how we felt about them at the time. Of course, the list will be extremely personal, but here are some examples of the kinds of things that might emerge:

- There were horrifying moments when my father was harshly critical of what he called 'being childish'. He'd say I was too old to have a teddy bear or to need to be tucked up in bed by my mother. I felt there was this stern, cold, mean way of being that he was forcing on me and that it was going to make me very unhappy.
- I got very upset – around maybe five – when my mother was going out to a party in the evening; she'd put on a special dress and I had this feeling she was abandoning me. There was this other world that was hostile to being cosy with me and she was saying, 'I don't want you, I want excitement'.
- When I was growing up, my mother didn't have much confidence; she used to get quite intimidated and she never felt she was good enough (particularly around my father's wider family). I felt such agonies on her behalf when I could see she felt hurt or put down.

- When I was a child, my parents conveyed the impression that sex was something very bad and disgusting.
- I remember standing alone in the playground at school. I didn't know how to join in; I was so frightened of everyone, I tried to pretend I didn't mind and that I wanted to be on my own.

Turn to the next page and fill out the table – as extensively and in as much detail as possible – with occasions in your own early life when you feel you were wounded emotionally. At this stage, we're simply acknowledging a difficult fact: we came into the relationship each carrying a difficult history of intimate emotional wounds, for which we deserve compassion and complex understanding.

Let's try to fill in this list in as much detail as possible:
Think about how you may have been emotionally wounded in your early life.

Let's try to fill in this list in as much detail as possible:

Think about how you may have been emotionally wounded in your early life.

Early Wounds

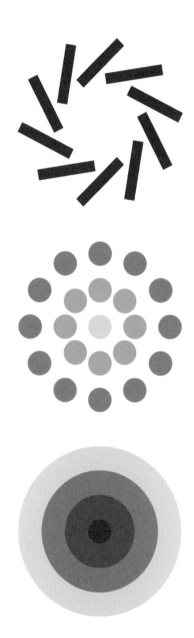

Part two: how our wounds show up today

Our early wounds set up patterns of behaviour that persist far into our adult lives. Without our necessarily realising it, they impacted on our development and slanted and distorted our character in various unfortunate ways.

There are a few big ways in which early hurts tend to show up later on.

We are hypersensitive

Our early experiences leave us acutely alert to certain things we perceived as threats, which to others might appear unalarming or unimportant. A mispronounced word, a hint of someone showing off, a lid left off a butter dish might be enough to set us deeply on edge – not because we are monstrous but because, owing to our emotional history, such apparently minor matters have been powerfully connected to very real dangers.

We over-compensate

We were let down in a key area and so maybe we go to extremes to make up for what we didn't get enough of. For instance, if there was too much chaos, we might become deeply invested in order and security; if we were bossed around too much, we might feel a huge need to assert our independence; if we always had to be very careful about money, we might get powerfully drawn to expensive luxuries.

We lack confidence

We developed the idea that there were quite stringent conditions attached to being found worthy of love: being overtly successful, being very 'good' or never complaining. Or maybe we feel that we can be acceptable only so long as we don't compete, or we fit in with the expectations of society, or we carefully disguise our interest in sex.

Take it in turns to complete the following sentences:

One thing I think I might be
hypersensitive about is ...

....

and I think this stems from ...

....

I think I probably
over-compensate in some
area's because of ...

....

An area in which I
lack confidence is ...

....

and I think this comes from ...

....

Take it in turns to complete the following sentences:

One thing I think I might be
hypersensitive about is ...

....

....

and I think this stems from ...

....

....

....

....

I think I probably
over-compensate in some
area's because of ...

....

....

An area in which I
lack confidence is ...

....

....

and I think this comes from ...

....

....

Early Wounds

14.
A New Ritual: The Morning and Evening Kiss

One of the constantly surprising aspects of relationships is just how much reassurance we need to believe that we are actively wanted – and, equally, how easy it is to forget this awkward fact both about ourselves and the other person.

The standard narrative of love tells us that insecurity about being wanted is going to be at its height at the start of the dating period, when we are acutely – and rather sweetly – conscious of the many ways in which our partner might not be keen on taking things further. But, we assume, once a relationship has started, once there might be children, a home and an established pattern of life, then surely the fear of being unwanted should disappear.

Far from it. The fear of being unwanted continues every day. There could always be new threats to love's integrity. Just because we were loved yesterday does not ensure a sense that we will be needed today. More perniciously, if a fear is left to fester, it can lead us to adopt a defensive position where, because we assume we are unwanted, we start to behave in a cold and detached way, which encourages the partner to act likewise. Two people who are, at heart, very well disposed towards one another, can end up in a cycle of each denying that they need the other, because they cautiously and pre-emptively assume that the other person no longer wants them.

In order to try to calm these fears and cycles of unwarranted detachment, we should be sure to institute an apparently small but, in fact, crucial ritual into our lives: a morning and evening kiss.

Every morning, before parting, no matter how much in a rush we both are, we should give one another a proper kiss on the lips, for at least seven seconds which is – in reality – a very strangely long time. Lean in close together, don't think about the many things you have to do in the hours ahead. Simply concentrate on the sensation of their mouth on yours, feel your nose against their skin. Don't break off abruptly at the end: Keep looking at each other for another few moments and give a smile. The same should be repeated every evening when you return home.

When we kiss we are tapping into a central channel of emotional connection. Intimate physical contact affects us in a way that's both distinct from, and in many ways superior to, words or ideas. We are sensuous creatures to at least the same degree as we are rational ones: A smile or a caress can therefore reassure us far more deeply than can an eloquent phrase or a well-articulated fact ('of course I love you …'). As babies we were soothed by touch long before we could understand language, and we therefore continue to need physical contact to believe, truly, that we have a place in another's life.

Normally a kiss follows from a tender feeling: We have an emotion first and then we express it. But there's another way our minds can work, a way in which a feeling follows from an action. The morning and evening kiss should hence come first, independently of whether or not there is as yet a tender emotion. But then, almost for certain, if we go through with the kiss, the emotion will occur (it's very hard to kiss and feel nothing). We may need to make that rather odd-sounding move in love: a small effort.

The morning and evening kiss should be a ritual. A central feature of rituals is that we do them whether we feel like doing them or not. The kiss should take place even if you've just had a rather sarcastic argument, or if you are racing to an important early meeting, or if you are feeling resentful. Better feelings will follow.

When leaving the house and heading to the station, we should no longer only ask whether we have remembered the keys or the report. We should always ask ourselves if we have done a far more crucial and love-sustaining thing: exchanged a seven-second kiss.

15.
Unconscious Belittling

In any relationship, even a very good one, two people will inevitably spend a fair amount of time criticising things that their beloved has said or done. We are – after all – fundamentally flawed creatures and we need to accept that we will have to learn a few things along the way, possibly every day. Maybe someone has forgotten to call the doctor. Perhaps someone needs to be reminded to set the alarm clock for slightly earlier …

The issue is not whether or not there will be criticism; what counts is the amount of sensitivity that two people can bring to the task. Some of the time at least, we end up deeply offending our partner even though we had no intention of doing so – while at other points, our remarks can be accepted in good faith and taken as constituting an important lesson.

It is, therefore, a priority to try to understand when we are belittling our partner, even when we did not mean to, and how we manage to aggravate our desire to impart a piece of helpful feedback. Our inner map of belittled feelings will be highly individual and normally connected with features of our past which need to be discovered and shared.

We will be hugely rewarded if we can take some time to share our maps of belittlement in a spirit of good faith.

Using the list below as a guide, ring any statements that remind you of times when you have felt your dignity seriously undermined.

These are things you can do to which I'm acutely sensitive (ring all the ones that resonate, then pick three to concentrate on):

talk over me

ask a question that's not linked to what I've just said

ask me to help and then criticise my efforts to assist you

talk with your friends about my career issues

mention my weight

tell me I'm being too sensitive about something

repeat something I told you was private to a friend

be a bit cold to me when in public or just before we go out

say everything is going to be fine, when I know it won't be

take the side of one of the children against me

fail to show sufficient appreciation of something I've paid for

agree with me just to keep the peace

seem uninterested in sex

say negative things about my parents

draw attention to what I'm wearing

don't mention what I'm wearing

give advice on driving, while I'm driving

comment on how I've mispronounced a word

tell me I'm over-reacting

ignore my hand when I reach over to touch you

sigh when I say something you don't agree with

don't engage with an argument I've just put forward

sulk

change the topic abruptly

praise me in a way that feels insincere

give me a 'joke' birthday present

ask me pointed questions about how things are going at work (I feel as if I'm being cross-examined)

don't ask me how my day went

ask me too many questions after I've been out with friends

emphatically do something that you
think I should have done already

hint at criticisms your
friends make of me

explain things slowly (so
'even I' will understand)

say there's no point in discussing
something with me

make a payment from our joint
account without telling me first

tell me how fascinating someone else is

comment admiringly on how
successful someone else is

tidy away something I'd
left out to use later

take lots of hand luggage onto a plane

try to get me to dance at a party

refuse to dance at a party

press me to stay too long at a party

press me to leave a party too early

reply very briefly when I've
sent you a longer message

check your phone while we're talking

laugh at something and then not
explain what was so funny

roll your eyes when I do
anything slightly clumsy

be unresponsive when I make
a suggestion around sex

be more charming to a stranger
than you usually are to me

don't hold my hand when
we're out together

don't notice when I've
made a special effort

try to use money to solve
an emotional problem

criticise my good friends

lean away from me when we're
sitting on the sofa together

imply I'm being hysterical
when I get upset

be cheerful when I'm feeling sad

There's a natural bias in our minds to see our partner as excessively fragile or over-sensitive around the things they find humiliating. When we look at their list, we're tempted to think: 'How can you let that get to you?' But when we do that we're forgetting that our own zones of potential humiliation can look equally excessive to them.

It's not that either of us is particularly weird. We're encountering in each other a standard feature of the human condition: that it's very easy for us to end up feeling slighted or under-valued – especially by the person to whom we've devoted our lives.

16.
The Anxious-Avoidant Quiz

We can usefully distinguish between two broad relationship styles: the anxious and the avoidant. Both the anxious and the avoidant person are in search of closeness, but they have different fears. The anxious person is worried that their partner will abandon them and so craves signs of warmth and affection and is panicked by any signs, real or imagined, of distance.

The avoidant person for their part wants to be close but is worried about rejection: They fear that if they reveal their emotional needs, they will be humiliated, so they come across as cold, distant and uninterested in connection.

To help identify whether you are anxious or avoidant (you may be neither!), try to answer the following questions:

If your partner doesn't respond to a request, do you ...
A.   nag them until they do what you've asked?
B.   feel you can't risk asking again?

Which statement feels more applicable to you?
A.   I wish we could spend more time together.
B.   I'd like more space in the relationship.

When you're feeling upset, do you instinctively ...
A.   want sympathy and a hug?
B.   want to be left to work through it on your own?

If your partner doesn't reply quickly to a message, do you ...
A.   worry about what they're up to – have they had an accident, or might they be having an affair?
B.   feel annoyed with them for being so inefficient?

You're invited to a party and your partner doesn't want to go. Do you ...
A.   insist that you can't go without them? You both go or neither of you goes.
B.   not mind? You'll have a nice time with your friends and, anyway, why should a couple do everything together?

Are you more likely to criticise your partner for being ...
A.   'too rational'?
B.   'too emotional'?

If your responses gravitate towards As, this suggests that you tend towards an anxious style of relating. If you generally answer with Bs, you're probably more the avoidant type.

It is very normal in a couple for one person to be more anxious and the other more avoidant – which is a cause of persistent misunderstandings. A way we can start to get around this is to imagine more carefully what is really going on in the mind of our partner.

If you are more anxious, try to complete the following statements as generously as you can and then discuss with your partner.

When you accuse me of nagging, you might be trying to tell me ...

When you seem offhand, you could be ...

When you want to be left alone, what's actually going on for you might be ...

If you are more avoidant, try to finish off these statements and then discuss with your partner.

When you strike me as intrusive, you might really be ...

When you seem clingy, what's actually motivating you could be ...

When you accuse me of not caring enough, what you are worried about might be ...

This is a moment for mutual compassion. Neither of you selected the emotional style you have; the style evolved under the various pressures you were exposed to as you were growing up. Sympathy and generosity are required.

There is an immense difference between acting on one's avoidant or anxious impulses and, as would be preferable, understanding that one has them, grasping where they came from and explaining to ourselves and others why they make us do what we do. We cannot – most of us – be wholly healthy in love, but we can be something almost as beneficial. We can grow into people committed both to explaining our unhealthy, trauma-driven behaviour in good time, before we have become overly furious and hurt others too much, and to apologising for our antics after they have run their course. There are few things more Romantic, in the true sense, than a couple who have learnt to tell one another with wit and composure that they have been triggered in an avoidant or an anxious direction, but are doing everything they can to get on top of things – and hope to be normal again in a little while.

17.
Projecting Emotions

It's a deep and powerful feature of our minds that we quickly interpret what's happening in a situation on the basis of a few slight clues. But, without realising it, we also sometimes smuggle in ideas which are more to do with us than with what's actually happening. This is called 'projection': We make an emotional assumption about others based on a hidden bias in our own experience.

We can catch sight of projection in action when we contemplate certain works of art and try to say what's going on in them.

Consider this portrait of a mother and daughter:

Jacques-Louis David, *Portrait of the Comtesse Vilain XIIII and her Daughter*, 1816

Different people might see this in very different ways. One person might say that the mother looks as if she's hardly interested in her daughter and seems quite cold and disengaged. Another person might feel that the mother is lost in tender but anxious thoughts: thinking how little her girl is and how large and complex and dangerous the world can be. Someone else could see the daughter as timid and clinging to her mother for reassurance, while another individual might say the daughter looks bored, as if her mother is holding her back from going off and doing whatever it is she'd rather be doing.

Historically speaking, we don't actually know anything about the relationship between this particular mother and daughter. The different ways of viewing it don't identify what was really going on between them; rather they reflect the inner emotional world of different viewers. Suppose, when we were little, we suffered because our own mother was often distracted and inattentive. The idea of a disengaged, melancholy mood will probably have grown more instinctive to us. Our minds are always seeking to refind this familiar emotional state – even if there isn't really too much evidence for it in the world. A tiny suggestive hint will be enough: Downcast eyes or a slightly tense mouth will be sufficient to make us feel sure that the other is withdrawn and sad, even if we don't really know what they are feeling at all. Similarly, if a parent was given to anxious foreboding, it will feel natural to us to see this woman as having these same kinds of thoughts. Or if as children we felt shy and fearful, we'll be primed to see the child in similar terms.

Or suppose we ourselves have often felt a desire to escape from overbearing demands – maybe from our parents, or from the constraints of education, or from the burdens of our working lives: The idea of being held back looms large in our minds. It comes to guide the way we interpret others. We may not have fully acknowledged our own sense of being trapped, but it's there in our souls and we project this feeling outwards and see others as being in a similar situation, even if they're not.

We can sometimes pick up on the projections others make of us, because we can see there's a real gap between what they feel sure we're doing and what we know we've done.

Sometimes my partner imagines I've done something on purpose to thwart them, when I haven't done anything at all. They can't find their car keys and they'll go, 'Why did you move my keys, why would you do that?', and they're on the verge of getting really angry – as you might if someone really had deliberately hidden your keys. But actually I haven't even touched them.

I get on quite well with my parents-in-law and I was texting them about having lunch with them over the weekend and my partner got the idea I was 'complaining about them' behind their back. I wasn't at all. If I meet up with friends, afterwards my partner will say, 'Did you talk about me?' It's as if they've got this picture of me in their heads that's not entirely connected to reality.

We can make sense of the idea of other people projecting, but it's harder to notice the phenomenon in our own case. We don't too often or too readily feel that we're taking our own past and using that to come to skewed interpretations of what's going on – and yet we may be …

To close in on your own patterns of projection, look at this picture:

Claude Monet, *Bazille and Camille (Study for
"Déjeuner sur l'Herbe")*, 1865

Individually, pick the statement that is closest to your own instinctive sense of what's going on with this couple:

A. They've just had a row and she wants to leave.

B. He's being domineering; she's upset but too intimidated to say anything.

C. She's being difficult; he's trying to understand, in order to help.

D. They're having a really interesting conversation; she's paused to gather her thoughts and he's just waiting to hear what she'll say next.

It's important to note that there's no correct interpretation of the picture: There's no external evidence at all about what they were saying or feeling. Take turns to consider what it might be in your own background that prompts you to see this couple the way you identified.

As a second exercise, take turns to complete the following sentences. Answer as quickly and spontaneously as possible; don't think it over, just give the first answer that comes to mind:

1. If a really good dancer sees someone floundering gracelessly on the dance floor, they probably think …

2. If you are wearing smart clothes and trip over in the street, the people around would probably …

3. You notice that someone driving a car is speaking on their phone – give a quick sketch of the kind of thing you imagine they're probably saying.

4. A middle-aged couple are sitting silently opposite each other at a table in a restaurant – what's the state of their relationship?

A key point here is that there could be multiple different answers that make perfect sense. A good dancer might be contemptuous of someone who can't dance at all, or they might be delighted to see someone having a go, or they might not think about them at all, or it might remind them of a beloved friend who has recently died. At the moment it doesn't matter what the statistical norm is (it may be, for instance, that sixty-three percent of good dancers feel contempt for those who can't dance) because this gives no precise guide to what is actually happening in any particular case.

What's at stake is what immediately comes to mind for you. This gives an approximate but revealing glimpse of the way you might be projecting onto others.

Take turns to try to explain, without being defensive, why you gave the answers you did.

Now try to identify occasions when, in your own relationship, you might be projecting onto one another. What unfortunate consequences follow from this?

We don't project because we are bad or stupid or unkind. We project because that is the way our minds function: We use familiar emotional patterns to imagine what's going on for others – though we'll sometimes get it very wrong. We'll imagine our partner is deliberately upsetting us when they aren't; we'll suppose they are angry with us when they're not; we will misconstrue their motives and moods. We make panicked, alarmist interpretations of what they are up to, not on the basis of reality but because of our own complex background emotional history.

18

Indirect Communication

We can all – humblingly – imagine how true adults in a relationship would ideally communicate. They would understand their own moods clearly, speak with confidence but without anger or bitterness, always wait for an appropriate moment to make their case, have faith that they will be heard and so not rush or force the issue and never raise their voices or start to cry.

Unfortunately, very little of this ever happens, for we are – most of us – only adults by chronological age rather than inner maturity. Instead of communicating directly and serenely, we tend to send out a variety of garbled, indirect, peculiar and very unhelpful signals about what's truly going on for us – signals that end up confusing, enraging and often boring our partner. We make it immensely hard for them to understand us with sympathy – and yet, at the same time, we profoundly resent their misunderstandings. This tragic loop is so undignified and painful that we're tempted to assume it must be unique. And yet, in the privacy of our homes, poor communication is the rule. We should try to understand the obstacles and look with sympathy and extreme compassion at how we could do better.

There are four big features of how our minds work that get in the way of sound communication:

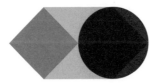

1. We assume that others should know

There is no more common belief in love than that the other person should understand what we want, feel, desire and are cross about without us needing to tell them. We carry with us a powerful idea that we can and should be read wordlessly or, to put it at its starkest, magically.

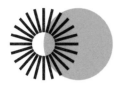

2. We panic

We get so scared that we won't be understood that we behave in ways that are guaranteed to confirm and exceed our worst fears. Rather than lay out our case calmly, terrified that we are wasting our life with someone who is committed to frustrating us, we lash out at the very worst moments (often late at night) and grow vindictive or self-pitying as we make our case.

We get bossy and controlling or perhaps silent and stern. At points, we immerse ourselves in our work or try to numb our pain with too much food or wine. What our partner witnesses is our outward behaviour, rather than the underlying distress, and so they assume that we're simply fussy or busy, sullen or self-indulgent. We lose the audience we so desperately need.

Being as honest and detailed as possible, both of you should complete the following sentence:
When I'm feeling anxious, I sometimes try to cope by …

This is the moment to give our partner a crucial guide to understanding us. We're putting into words what we usually express only through misleading behaviour. We're admitting to the troubles that underlie our more unfortunate and foolish actions.

3. We seek attention in regrettable ways

We want our partner to turn their mind generously and sympathetically to what's bothering us, but instead of quietly explaining, we employ indirect – and sometimes dramatic – strategies. Even an act as apparently dismissive as storming out of a room can be a plea for understanding (though delivered in a way that is certain to fail).

4. We sulk

A sulk is one of the more peculiar varieties of indirect communication. We both refuse to say what is bothering us in a polite and kind way – and at the same time perversely hope that our partner will understand what's wrong and be wholly kind and sympathetic to our cause.

When our partner asks what's the matter, we say, very gruffly, 'I'm fine, nothing's wrong'. But what we truly mean is: 'You should already have understood what you've done wrong and what's upsetting me. I'm hoping you'll now notice and apologise with great kindness, but I'm going to make sure you don't so that I can prove how unkind you are.' It sounds absurd – and it is.

Try to recall a particular occasion of sulking and explain to your partner:

A. why you got upset

B. what you felt

C. why it was so hard for you to say it directly

The origins of indirect communication almost always lie in childhood. When we were very young, we often didn't have the capacity or context to understand and explain what was upsetting us, so we resorted to saying nothing, to hating silently, to having tantrums and to stamping our feet. Think about the following questions and discuss with your partner:

What did you learn about communication from your parents?

What did they do when they were upset?

Were you helped to find the words?

What role models did you have?

What were you allowed to do with your upset and angry moods?

Ideally, when faced with a miscommunicating partner, we'd do our utmost to read between the lines. We'd understand that, at times, they wouldn't be able to tell us (or would feel too agitated to tell us) what was actually wrong and so would behave in ways that sent muddled, unkind, indirect messages about their inner state. We'd appreciate that behind their tantrums lay desperate and disorganised attempts to be lovingly understood.

But when we were truly feeling a little stronger, we would realise that the burden is ultimately on us both to learn to level our complaints in a way that is slightly more sober, serene and kind.

Sympathise with the difficulties of being mature (even if you are at an advanced age).

1. Pick a topic that often upsets and enrages you.

2. Practise laying out your case directly and maturely.

3. Reverse and repeat.

Fill out the table on the next page together, picking the entries that are most relevant to you.

When I …

1. It might seem that …

2. But, what I really mean is …

nag you

suddenly lose my temper

criticise you for …

have a very long bath

flirt with someone else

stay on my phone

When I …	1. It might seem that …	2. But, what I really mean is …
nag you		
suddenly lose my temper		
criticise you for …		
have a very long bath		
flirt with someone else		
stay on my phone		

Indirect Communication

19.
A Better Kind of Evening

Over the years, we will have spent a huge number of evenings at home together, but we tend to fall into routines and habits that mean that we cease to be very ambitious about what can be achieved. Mostly we're not having a terrible time, but we could get a lot more thoughtful too.

We can usefully ask ourselves what a really good ordinary evening might look like. We're not thinking just about what we'd individually like but what we think we'd enjoy together based on precedent; and we're not examining our fantasies of the absolutely ideal evening, we're thinking about what's realistically manageable given who we both are – something that could become a new routine on a regular basis.

There are a few basic dimensions to consider:

What to eat
What we eat subtly influences our mood – we might foreground comfort or simplicity or adventure; we could prepare something that reminds us of a particular holiday or that one of us associates with the happier aspects of childhood.

Timing
At what point does our evening start? What needs to be out of the way first? What time should we be going to bed? We can get quite detailed here: If we're cooking, what time do we need to put the oven on? How late should we stay up?

Conversation
What might we talk about and are there topics it might be best to deliberately avoid?

Space vs. togetherness
How much do we want to be closely interacting? Is it OK to have phones? Can we, at points, use different rooms?

We solicited ideas from our community. Here are some suggestions people made about their ideal evening with their partner:

The washing up: Can we do as much of it as possible in advance and make sure the kitchen is tidy before we sit down to eat? I find it jarring to have a pile of pots and pans to face at the end of the meal; if there's just a couple of plates and a few pieces of cutlery, it's not so bad.

I'd like to play a card game.

Could we have a drink before the meal – even just for five minutes? For me, it always creates a slight sense of occasion.

What if we start a bit later – like 9 p.m. – so I could get any work things I need to do out of the way, rather than trying to do them after?

Could we make a pact not to talk about work?

How about if we agree not to check our phones (we could dig out our watches so we can check the time)?

I want to be with you but not talk too much.

I want us to talk more about our dreams and regrets.

I want to be sad with you.

We'd read in bed for about half an hour at the end (I'd like an extra pillow to support my neck).

On the next page, each of you should separately make your own sketch of the ideal evening, then see if you can come up with a joint plan. If there are areas you can't quite agree on, try both on different occasions. Agree on at least two dates to put your plans into action.

My ideal evening with my partner:

20.
How I Am Difficult to Live With

We don't need people to be perfect. What we need – above all – is a sense that they understand their imperfections, that they are ready to explain them to us and that they can do so outside of the moments when they have hurt us.

It's a sign of being a grown-up that we can, finally, admit that we are really quite difficult to live with. Everyone is. It's just a question of how we, in particular, are tricky.

We might, for instance, have very strong views about interior design and find any opposition to our taste quite distressing. We might be fanatically (and often anxiously) devoted to our work. We could have strong views on how long it is OK to keep a taxi waiting, whether bedroom windows should be kept open at night or what time a child needs to go to bed (to start sketching a potentially endless list).

Recognising where we are inflexible and where we are very demanding won't solve all the points of contention. But it can hugely and decisively change the atmosphere. We should both never be done with the business of recognising and (gently) apologising for how challenging we are to be around.

Each name five ways in which you are quite difficult to live with:

1.

2.

3.

4.

5.

1.

2.

3.

4.

5.

21.
A Forgiveness Ritual

We do bad and unthoughtful things all the time, of course. But generally, we tell ourselves that we're not to blame and, indeed, that it's our partner who should be apologising – and asking *us* to forgive *them*. But in our more honest moments, we all recognise that we have unfairly brought certain troubles into the relationship. It would be strange if we hadn't. We are complex individuals; we're not remotely perfect in every way. We mess up daily.

Unfortunately, when we feel guilty – but are unforgiven – we have a tendency to get aggressive and deny all our flaws. We therefore need to create an atmosphere where an admission of guilt will be met with tolerance and sympathy. We're not asking the other person to wipe the slate clean. We're signalling that we want to do better, if we're given the chance.

We tend to deny our errors out of fear that if we own up to them, the other will be catastrophically angry or we'll be unfairly exploited. To lessen the anxiety, confessions therefore need to be mutual, candid, measured and undertaken with immense goodwill and generosity on both sides.

The people we most hurt are always those we most love; not out of deliberate malice, but because, by being close, we are exposing one another to the most vulnerable parts of our natures, where our frailties and errors take on a monstrous potential to cause harm.

Close up, it's horrible, but from a cosmic distance we deserve almost infinite compassion for our sorrows and our shame – to which we are condemned simply by being human and by sharing our daily lives with another person.

Things I wish I hadn't done that I'd love you to forgive me for:

Particular occasions

Patterns of behaviour

Troubles I have brought
into your life

Things I wish I hadn't done that I'd love you to forgive me for:

Particular occasions

....

....

....

....

....

....

....

....

Patterns of behaviour

....

....

Troubles I have brought
into your life

....

....

A Forgiveness Ritual

22.
A Gratitude Ritual

We're so conscious of the areas of tension in the relationship, we tend to forget – day to day – all the enormous ways in which our partner has helped us to grow and to feel safe. This person may be both the most maddening person we have ever known and at the same time, deep down, the person to whom we're most profoundly grateful.

They made it possible to do things we'd never have accomplished on our own: They have comforted us at moments of extreme crisis; they've maybe understood and been kind to difficult aspects of who we are; possibly they have saved us from the worst effects of certain tendencies in our nature.

We might fear that if we exhibited gratitude, our partner would get irritated. They might think: 'If you're so grateful to me, why do you behave so badly to me?' We might fear that we'd come across as sly and insincere – as if we were only saying something that sounded very nice in order to boost our negotiating position in some other upcoming area. Or we might be fearful that if we assured our partner of our appreciation, they would take our goodwill for granted, start exploiting us, stop making any effort – and leave us with far fewer things to be grateful for.

All these reasons for not expressing gratitude are deeply understandable – but they share a common flaw: They don't, when we think about it, apply to us personally. That is, we're attributing to our partner states of mind that we don't ourselves have – and that no one else does either. In fact, if they expressed gratitude to us, we'd be pleasantly surprised; we wouldn't feel that they were stating the obvious. We wouldn't be angry, we wouldn't take advantage of their goodwill and we wouldn't cynically assume they were trying to put us off our guard.

Finish the following sentences, explaining something you are grateful for.
Be specific, go into detail:

You've taught me ...

....

You've shown me ...

....

You've introduced me to ...

....

You've comforted me when ...

....

You've given me a better understanding of ...

....

You've made me less afraid of ...

....

You've supported me around ...

....

Because of you, I have been able to ...

....

Without you I'd have struggled to ...

....

Thank you for ...

....

Finish the following sentences, explaining something you are grateful for.
Be specific, go into detail:

You've taught me ...

You've shown me ...

You've introduced me to ...

You've comforted me when ...

You've given me a better understanding of ...

You've made me less afraid of ...

You've supported me around ...

Because of you, I have been able to ...

Without you I'd have struggled to ...

Thank you for ...

A Gratitude Ritual

23.
Our Conspiracy

At the start, a relationship can – in the best way – feel a little like a conspiracy against the rest of the world. They, the others, those not blessed enough to be part of this unique, enchanted club, are on the outside: They don't get the jokes, they can't understand the allusions, they don't get the right music or clothes, they aren't quite as clever or as wicked or as down to earth. They certainly don't know what really great sex is. At the end of parties, we retire to our private cocoon and discuss how – in so many ways – other people really didn't come up to scratch and therefore, by implication, how perfect we are. It sounds a little mean and, in a sense, it is. But the feeling of conspiracy is a vital glue. It serves to build up some of the loyalty that a couple needs to get going and define itself. This feeling of conspiracy helps to form two 'I's into a 'we'.

But in time, the conspiratorial glue can weaken. We may forget what sets us nicely apart. We may – indeed – start to look outwards with longing, wondering what they, the others, have that we don't.

So it pays to take a little time to remind ourselves of the reasons why we were and continue to be a bit special, a couple not like everyone else, privy to an understanding of things that others can't so easily 'get'.

We're taught so much about why a feeling of superiority is wrong that we forget to notice how it may, in certain contexts, play an important role in solidifying our sense of why we still belong together.

Think of ways in which, in a range of areas, you have something that a lot of other people don't quite have; ways in which you are a bit set apart and are (in a quiet way) slightly better than the rest.

What do we really see eye to eye on when it comes to:

who is an interesting person

what friends to pick

who is a bore

what good art is

how to decorate a home

how to raise children

what good sex can be

how to think about politics

how to have fun

what the best values are

24.
Admiration

We forget this, of course. But we still admire bits of one another quite a lot.

Maybe we're impressed by how nicely our partner keeps their wardrobe, or by how they are good at making a decision and following through; perhaps we're struck by their confidence around administrative tasks, or we're slightly in awe of their planning skills; maybe we admire their ability to brush off minor mishaps, or the way they don't get easily intimidated by creative challenges.

Each of you should now list, in as much detail as possible, what you admire about your partner. It can feel like a very odd exercise, after all the bickering, but the lists are life-saving. You might want to frame them and put them on the wall, to consider after moments of tension.

What I still admire in you:

-
-
-
-
-
-

What I still admire in you:

-
-
-
-
-
-

25.
The Weakness of Strength

After spending time around our partner for years, what can dominate our awareness of them is their flaws: how rigid they can be, how muddled, self-righteous, vague or proud. We grow into experts in their deficiencies of character.

We should, in our most impatient and intemperate moments, strive to hold on to the concept of the Weakness of Strength. This dictates that we should interpret people's weaknesses as the inevitable downside of certain merits that drew us to them, and from which we will benefit at other points (even if none of these benefits are apparent right now). What we're seeing is not their faults, pure and simple, but rather the shadow side of things that are genuinely good about them. If we were to write down a list of strengths and then of weaknesses, we'd find that almost everything on the positive side of the ledger would be connected up with something on the negative. The theory urges us to search a little more assiduously than is normal for the strength with which a maddening characteristic must be twinned. We can see easily enough that someone is pedantic and uncompromising; we tend to forget, at moments of crisis, their thoroughness and honesty. We know so much about a person's messiness, we have forgotten their uncommon degree of creative enthusiasm. The very same character trait that we approve of will be inseparable from tendencies we will end up regretting. This isn't bad luck or the case with just one or two people; it's a law of nature. There can, perplexingly, be no such thing as a person with only strengths.

It's a standard, and maddening, perversity of human nature that our merits and our admirable qualities always bring quite specific drawbacks with them. The fact that someone is strong and impressive in one area almost always entails that they will be weak and annoying in another rather precise way.

The theory of the Weakness of Strength invites us to be calm and forensic around the most irritating aspects of those we live with. There is no comfort in being told that these aspects are not real or significant. The consolation comes in not viewing them in isolation; in remembering the accompanying trait that redeems them and explains the relationship; in recalling that a lack of time management might have its atonement in creativity, or that dogmatism might be the offshoot of precision.

It is always an option to move away and find lovers who will have new kinds of strength, but – as time will reveal – they will also have new, fascinating and associated kinds of weakness.

Enduring love is built out of a constantly renewed and gently resigned awareness that weakness-free people do not exist.

Emotionally, such a table has an important meaning: that we're never going to be able to get the good things we like about our partner without also meeting various closely linked problems; and they are going to face the same problem with us.

But instead of their defects being cast in a purely negative light, their flaws can be seen as part of the cost of their virtues. Their strengths and weaknesses emanate from the same psychological core – which also suggests how hard it might be for our partner to eradicate some of their failings without also undercutting the qualities we admire them for. The Weakness of Strength explains why there is no perfect partner for us: Finding someone who is very reliable might also mean finding someone who is a touch boring; a partner who is thoroughly responsible around money might very likely also strike us as not very generous. The frictions and frustrations of our relationship are not just a matter of individual bad luck; they derive, in significant part, from the very foundations of human nature.

Now, individually, think about your partner's good qualities and consider what – objectively speaking – are the probable weaknesses that go along with these strengths.

In the table on the next page, each make a list of your partner's good qualities and the likely related weaknesses that go along with them.

Appealing strength:	Probable weakness:
Very organised	Will get frustrated, bossy, impatient
Patient/relaxed	Will be at points lackadaisical and dilatory; will not see the urgency; perhaps not so tidy
Very sensible/reliable around money	Will appear 'materialistic' and not sufficiently alive to the spirit
Sexy, confident in their allure, erotically playful	May have a tendency to flirt
Industrious, focused, successful around work	Will appear preoccupied by work, anxious and awkward on holiday

Probable weakness:

Appealing strength:

Probable weakness:

The Weakness of Strength

26.
Hidden Efforts

There are quite often times when we do little things, inspired by a kindly or generous motive towards our partner, which for lots of reasons we end up not mentioning. Maybe our action feels too minor, maybe we just forget, perhaps we think it is obvious to them. But in reality our partner might very well not be aware of our smaller acts of consideration: not because they are insensitive, but because our kindly move or sweet thought has been going on behind the scenes. It's a pity that these get missed because our partner is usually very aware of all the less than lovely things we do, so their picture of us, and of our attitude to them, is lopsided to a certain degree. And, of course, this is a mutual loss.

As a corrective, we can try to list explicitly some of the little efforts we've made out of goodwill or in homage to each other. To get a flavour of the kinds of things that might go on the list, here are some that were mentioned in The School of Life head office when we were road-testing this exercise.

> *One time I was getting into the car to go to the shops and I remembered my partner had been mentioning that they didn't like the way people used so many plastic bags, so I went back into the house and got a cotton bag – I forgot to say anything about it later. Actually, it's happened a few times.*

> *I was getting dressed and I was going to put on my grey trousers, but I put on the brown ones instead because I think my partner prefers me in them.*

> *I've started polishing the lenses of my glasses more often – a while back my partner pointed out how they sometimes looked a bit dirty; I hadn't really noticed it myself.*

> *When I'm buying chocolate I usually get the very dark kind (I like it but it's not my own first choice) because I know it's my partner's favourite.*

I was making them a cup a tea and I was about to grab the nearest cup when I thought they'd prefer the blue-and-white one, so that was the one I gave them instead.

Yesterday evening I was cooking and my partner was setting the table and I was going to point out that they'd forgotten to put salt and pepper on the table, but I didn't say anything – I just quietly and calmly went to the cupboard and got them myself.

A while back my partner mentioned that I chew too loudly. I didn't react well at the time, but later I thought they might have a point. I actually try to chew more carefully now – though I suppose I sometimes forget.

Individually, draw up your own list on the page overleaf, then show it to your partner.

The hidden efforts I make for you:

The hidden efforts I make for you:

27.
Undelivered Compliments

There are things we like about our partner and ways they've helped us that we don't get around to mentioning. The gratitude and admiration is there in our head but it's not transmitted – so our partner's idea of what we make of them is unfortunately skewed.

Without really thinking about it, we often tend to assume that if someone is doing something well, they must be fully aware of it themselves – and know we must be pleased. But from our own experience we can see that this isn't true. We don't go around confidently feeling that our partner has a very positive view of many things we do, if they never mention it; rather we assume they haven't noticed or don't care.

Here are some compliments various people in The School of Life community hadn't paid their partners:

I really like the way my partner parks the car in tight spaces: confident, quick, precise, no fuss – even if there's just a few centimetres at each end.

They've got a lopsided smile, which I like a lot. It comes out especially when they're laughing at something slightly idiotic they've done.

Two years ago they repainted the bedroom walls. I was unsure about it at the time, but the colour has grown on me – now I really like it. I don't think I've actually mentioned it.

They've got the perfect case for their phone: black suede.

They've got really nice shoulders – it's weird to say, but I probably haven't told them since the first few weeks we were together.

I really like that they are friends with my sister.

They always have a stash of replacement light bulbs somewhere in the house; it's maybe only once a year that I need one, but it's really nice that they're there.

Individually, draw up your own list on the next page, then show it to your partner.

Compliments I forgot to pay you:

Compliments I forgot to pay you:

Undelivered Compliments

28.
How to Complain

Complaining carries such negative connotations that it can be hard to remember that there are better and worse ways of doing it – and, indeed, hard to realise that an essential ingredient of love is to know how to level complaints kindly.

So many of our critical thoughts are legitimate but are let down by the method of their delivery. We nag, we harangue, we attack, we rant, we make cutting, sarcastic remarks, all of which make our partner deny and escape rather than investigate how they might learn.

Complaining is a skill. Typically, if we haven't carefully practised a complicated task (like playing the violin or reversing an articulated lorry), we'll do it very badly; but in principle it can be done successfully, if we develop the relevant skills. So, too, with complaining. The notion of a skill is generous to the inadequacy of our natural instincts. It proposes that many important tasks will be beyond us, unless we undergo a period of training.

In this spirit, here is a short guide to how to complain well:

One: layer criticism with reassurance

Any criticism (as we know when we're on the receiving end) feels like a withdrawal of love. Therefore, it's extremely helpful to convey great admiration and respect as we're announcing our negative insight.

> I love giving you a kiss, but there's just this one tiny thing: It's even nicer when you've just brushed your teeth.

As opposed to:

> You know, your breath stinks. It's disgusting.

> You are so lovely and I can't help imagining other people finding you attractive. Don't blame me for being selfish: I want to keep you to myself.

As opposed to:

> Why the hell were you flirting with that idiotic person?

Two: make it clear that it's normal, and understandable, for your partner to have this failing

One of the things we are primed to resent is being made to feel freakish or being negatively compared to others who are 'good', while (obviously) we are 'bad'.

> No-one on the planet has to put up with this; why can't you see that obviously it was your turn to take the bins out?

Or, alternatively:

> Taking the bins out is obviously about the most boring task imaginable. I can't imagine anyone not wanting to get out of it, but it occurs to me that maybe yesterday it was actually your turn.

> You've become probably the least imaginative person in the world in bed. Martin and Jannine are fucking like crazy; what's wrong with you?

Or, alternatively:

> I don't know anyone whose sex life has stood the test of time, but maybe we could slightly buck the trend?

Three: use qualifiers – maybe, perhaps, possibly, by chance

Often what we hate about criticism is its directness. In a secret part of our minds we're not inherently unwilling to accept that we're very far from perfect – but we can't bear having certain truths stated to us bluntly. Compare:

> I hate the way you try to tell a story; you're like a demented robot that's got no idea what needs to be explained first, what's an irrelevant detail or what the point of the whole thing is.

With:

> It sometimes seems to me that maybe you haven't entirely got in focus the reaction you are hoping to elicit from others.

> You are such a revolting snob, I want to die of shame when I hear you pontificating in front of other people.

With:

> I wonder if it's just possible that at times not everyone fully identifies with the interesting point you are making.

Four: explain what is genuinely at stake for you

We don't realise it, but often our criticism doesn't perfectly target the real source of our distress. We lash out, we condemn our partner in their whole being, rather than surgically addressing a very precise problem. We might say:

> When you were slightly abrupt with my mother, it made me unhappy. I totally understand: She's not your best friend and she can be pretty annoying. But I feel I have to be loyal to her; I can't emotionally afford to alienate her more than I already have. I hardly dare ask, but I'd love you to grit your teeth and be sweet with her – I know its a lot to ask, but it would mean so much to me.

Rather than:

> You're a bitch/bastard.

> It's pretty difficult to explain, but I have this quite intense thing about cutlery. I know it sounds weird, but it does bother me when the knives and forks don't match. Ultimately, I suppose matching means harmony for me. It's a little detail that speaks about a grand theme. When you bought those new knives I know you were thinking they were a bargain – but would you mind very much if we kept them in reserve? Maybe on Saturday we can go and look for some others.

Rather than:

> You've ruined my whole life.

Five: reveal the longing beneath the complaint

Quite often, when we complain, there's a vulnerable part of us that wants to be recognised, appreciated and looked after. But we're understandably nervous about revealing our deepest hopes. So instead we go on the attack. We opt for:

> You promised you'd be here at seven and it's seven fourteen. You drive me mad.

But don't dare admit:

> I was counting down the time till you got here. I'm so excited and nervous that we've got this time just to ourselves; I worry that I'm keener on you than you are on me. I so want things to go well, that's why I'm agitated – a few minutes doesn't really matter.

> Did you really pay that for a haircut? I can't believe how vain you are.

But don't dare admit:

> I'm worried that you don't think I'm attractive, so when I see you taking an interest in your own appearance it makes me feel you are too good for me. I feel very unsure about being liked or found interesting or appealing and I want you to understand this about me.

In each pair of statements the underlying criticism is exactly the same but it is delivered in radically different ways.

Taking turns, each imagine you are an actor trying out for two different roles in a film. In one you'll be cast as a harsh critic and in the other you'll be skilled at delivering a critique surely but with minimal hostility. The film is based generically on your life as a couple. There are two versions for each scene: one in which the harsh critic appears and one in which the gentle, skilled critic has a starring role.

If you can bear to, pick out for the director a few criticisms you've each recently had of each other and play out the scenes using the two divergent characters.

- How would the harsh critic announce what they're unhappy about?
- How might the skilled critic speak?

29.
A Pessimistic Interlude

Many books that are, superficially, a bit like this one are laced with optimism. They promise that everything will be OK, and that relationships can, fundamentally, be rendered pain free. We aren't of this view.

Even if you were to follow every exercise to this point, there will still be times when you will feel very bleak about your relationship. Those moments won't necessarily last long, but they are bound to arise – and they are normal.

Here, therefore, are some bits of stiff, kindly consolation for the periods of agony.

Why did you get together with this person?
How did you get it so wrong?

In short: It's not your fault. Everyone, when known properly, turns out to be unbearable in some central ways. There is no one you could be with who would not, at times, leave you feeling desperate. You, too, are tricky, you should remember.

Many people suffer in similar ways now, have done so in the past and will do so again in the future. It's miserable, but you are participating in the common experience of humanity. Maybe they don't talk about it much, but millions would sympathise deeply with what you're going through. You feel completely alone, yet you are in a vast (shy) majority.

A thoughtful, well-read surgeon screamed at his partner through the bathroom door late last night and woke the children. Right now, a level-headed, nicely dressed IT consultant lives in dread of her partner finding out she's been having an affair online.

No one really understands anyone else. That your partner doesn't grasp you in central ways is entirely unavoidable.

Your anguish is very real at this moment. But later it won't seem quite so bad. We get used to things. We can cope better than we think.

We rightly put a lot of thought and effort into trying to make things better. But there's a strangely cheering thought that comes from a very different direction: pessimism. It's the acceptance that, whatever we try, our life together will still contain friction, conflict, awkwardness and pockets of mutual incomprehension. Pessimism isn't the idea that our specific relationship is doomed; on the contrary, it's a universal, philosophical point of view that admits early on that the human condition is horribly flawed. Things turn out quite badly not because we've made some specific mistake or because we weren't clever or skilful or lucky enough, but rather because the task is essentially beyond us: we're two radically imperfect, oddly complicated creatures with limited self-knowledge, multiple conflicting desires and needs, carrying the burdens of our past, who evolved from lizards and apes – so of course it's going to be incredibly arduous for us to live together harmoniously.

Pessimism is consoling because it foregrounds how the laws of existence are stacked against us and therefore invites us to be unshocked and unsurprised when things, inevitably, go badly. Constructive pessimism doesn't come naturally to us. But certain works of art, and certain aphorisms, put us in touch with it or renew its reassuring force in our minds. In a nineteenth-century painting by Jean-Baptiste-Camille Corot (see overleaf), we're drawn towards a melancholy mood: a solitary boatman is tying his small craft to a withered tree at the side of a gloomy lake; a couple of figures are huddled in the rough grass; the overcast afternoon is dying away; darkness is coming. Nothing wonderful or exciting is ever going to happen, but it's bearable – life will go on repetitively and quietly. We're looking at a particular scene, but we're seeing a metaphor for existence: muted, grey and modest.

Jean-Baptiste-Camille Corot, *The Boatman of Mortefontaine*, 1865–1870

Why cry over a part of life, when the whole of it calls for tears? – Seneca

We have begun to know someone properly whenever they have started substantially to disappoint us.

No one has ever properly understood me, I have never fully understood anyone; no one understands anyone else. – Goethe

Choosing a person to marry is just a matter of deciding what particular kind of suffering we would like to commit ourselves to.

The only people we can think of as normal are those we don't yet know very well.

The greatest part of our suffering is brought about by our hopes (for health, happiness and success). Therefore, the kindest thing we can do for ourselves is to recognise that our griefs are not incidental or passing, but a fundamental aspect of existence which will only get worse – until the worst of all happens.

30.
How to Argue

We all hate having arguments so much that there can be a reluctance to make our peace with them and accept that they are an inevitable feature of a life together – and, therefore, that the real challenge is to learn how to argue well rather than not argue at all.

A good argument is one in which we can get another person to understand and appreciate what is truly bothering us without upsetting or humiliating them overly. Even if we don't end up entirely agreeing, we should at least grasp each other's point of view – and accept the legitimacy of a contrary perspective.

There is a range of factors that get in the way of having a 'good' argument:

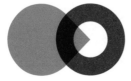

One: we ignore our broader psychological state
When we're tired or hungry or when we've been hurt by the world or hate ourselves, we can't be in a good state to convey our more complex needs and thoughts in a reasonable way. The surrounding distress too easily gets channelled into the argument.

We should study when we typically argue and try to identify what it might be about those times that predisposes us to be agitated. For instance, a couple might quite often argue in the car, late at night, after seeing friends or in the presence of their children.

When do we tend to argue?

What broader circumstances, for one or both of us, might be feeding the argument?

Two: we make global criticisms rather than precise statements
When we're upset, we habitually attack the whole being of our partner. We don't restrict ourselves to a local offence; we say they're selfish or lazy, mean or stupid. We don't mean it truly; we're simply unable to pinpoint the true nature of our upset.

Global criticism I tend to make of you:

Global criticism I tend to make of you:

What specifically bothers me:

What specifically bothers me:

Three: we have an unfortunate argument style

There are a few basic styles of unfortunate argument. Look through the list and see which ones you recognise:

A. *The person who doesn't dare to say directly what they mean*

For instance, they may actually be annoyed by how their partner dominates things financially, but they feel embarrassed to address this head on, so they get confrontational about doing the washing up or about their partner's taste in shoes. The energy of the confrontation is coming from somewhere else.

B. *The person who tries desperately to win the argument*

Emotionally, they're more invested in being 'right' (that is, making the other person submit) than in finding a resolution to a problem. In the background, long before the relationship started, they probably had some very negative experiences around being verbally or intellectually humiliated; they want to make sure that if there is humiliation at play this time around, they will be the one doling it out.

C. *The person who tries to inflict guilt*

When they argue they are trying to make their partner feel bad about themselves; at the back of their minds they have an idea that feeling ashamed is what makes people reform themselves.

D. *The person who acts passive-aggressively*

They don't overtly seem to be seeking an argument at all, but they do things that they sense will provoke their partner to make a criticism, which they can then cast as unfair and exaggerated. They do not have the courage of their underlying anger.

E. The person who blows their top, then feels they're a monster
They get enraged and at the same time know that shouting means they've lost. At the root of this behaviour is a strange-sounding idea: This person has no confidence that their complaints could be properly heard and reasonably responded to if they stayed calm.

F. The person who insists they don't care
They deny that the issue that agitates their partner is any business of theirs. They don't entirely believe this, but they feel it's too risky to get involved. They like to think that they are reasonable and their partner is 'mad'.

It can feel awkward to pick out a difficult argument style and admit that it's our own, though in fact practically everyone argues in one or other of these ways. Simply acknowledging the issue might in itself be of significant help to our partner. But, additionally, if we can bear to identify what we're like when we're angry, we can begin to think about how we might like to amend our way of engaging with conflict.

How might one change? Here are some suggestions for how to reform one's approach:

A. The person who doesn't dare to say directly what they mean
I might have grown up in an environment where no one spoke their anger and disappointment, but I now commit myself to using words and to delivering them calmly at an appropriate moment. I have a right – and indeed a duty – to speak and to say what is truly bothering me, rather than landing on a convenient but deceptive decoy.

B. The person who tries desperately to win the argument
I have to remind myself that the ultimate goal is to make the relationship better.

C. The person who tries to inflict guilt
I have to keep in mind that guilt never leads to change; I don't myself respond positively to being made to feel guilty, and I can extend the same insight to my partner. The idea is to change someone's mind by increasing their sense of hope and by engaging their enthusiasm.

D. *The person who acts passive-aggressively*

I can be assertive and still be an acceptable human being. There's a major difference between being vicious and simply stating one's case. My experience in my early past isn't a good guide to what I should be doing with my partner.

E. *The person who blows their top, then feels they're a monster*

I can learn to be more simple and straightforward in mentioning that I'm unhappy about something; my partner doesn't want me to be miserable. They may not be able to accommodate what I want, but they probably will understand if I explain my upset and frustration.

F. *The person who insists they don't care*

I can admit that I do care but that I'm frightened you'll use my caring to exploit me. I need to trust that I can care and say 'no' at the same time.

Four: we don't identify what we're really arguing about
We might be furiously disputing whose turn it is to take out the bins or whether driverless cars have a big future, but behind the scenes the real confrontation is elsewhere.

Think of as many times as possible when you've argued. What were the overt topics? List them as best you can in the left-hand column of the table on the next page.

Then fill in the right-hand column. There are so many overt matters over which couples come into conflict, but beneath the surface there may be only a small number of fundamental issues that get – indirectly – addressed in a thousand squabbles. See where the following six will fit:

i.   I don't feel understood.
ii. I don't feel in control.
iii. I don't have enough space.
iv. I don't feel successful.
v.   I don't feel close to you.
vi. I don't feel sexually desired.

Make a list of the issues you may have been indirectly arguing about.
Pay particular attention to the right-hand column, using the list i-vi on page 161.

What we 'officially' argued about: What we might truly have been arguing about:

Make a list of the issues you may have been indirectly arguing about.
Pay particular attention to the right-hand column, using the list i–vi on page 161.

What we 'officially' argued about:

_____

What we might truly have been arguing about:

_____

How to Argue

31.
Concrete Change

We often carry around with us a large set of wishes about how we'd like our partner to change. We might, for example, like them to be less bossy or more organised, more creative or less argumentative.

Each list a few of the key ways in which you'd like the other person to change:

1.

2.

3.

4.

1.

2.

3.

4.

These wishes could be entirely legitimate and important, but it pays to notice one key thing about them: They are often very vague and rather general.

In order for change to become a reality, we need to get a lot more concrete in our demands – and to state where exactly change could be enacted in the course of a typical day, rather than in the context of a whole personality. So rather than dreamily longing that the partner become 'more affectionate', we could – for example – specify that we would, all this week, like our partner to hold our hand in the evening in front of the television while the news is on. Or, instead of proposing that our partner 'grow more attentive', we could agree that we want to carve out ten minutes of proper conversation with them at least two mornings a week.

Change is always hard, but it is particularly so when we trade only in abstractly formulated demands. We need to make change feel a lot more concrete and context rich. We should also keep our demands at the modest end of the spectrum. We won't realistically manage overnight to transform our partner into a paragon of emotional warmth, but we might succeed in changing the way they greet us when we come back from work tomorrow. We can't expect someone to become more family minded in an instant, but it would be a great start if they agreed to see our mother on Tuesday. We should identify the smallest possible alteration that could nevertheless adequately signal to us that our partner was moving in the right direction.

Go back through the demands on page 164 and, in each case, indicate what a single, modest, concrete change would look like in that area.

Then, from your partner's answers, pick one change that you think you might be able to manage. The ideal is to make a few mutual agreements: 'If you do one minimal thing for me, I'll do one for you'.

You won't transform each other, but that was never on the cards. You'll be doing something far more realistic and, in its way, ambitious: helping each other to grow, concrete step by concrete step.

32.
Change is Possible

Because change is so hard, we can easily lose hope (and therefore become aggressive and sullen). We need, therefore, regularly to remind ourselves that change is possible and that people do – in fact – alter, with enough time, love and a good headwind.

To make this idea vivid, we should take time to talk to one another about how we have ourselves already changed in a range of areas. Over the years, our individual preferences, interests, habits, outlook, priorities, manners, conversational styles, enthusiasms, worries and values will almost certainly have shifted, sometimes very dramatically. One of the most useful things we can know about each other (and about ourselves) is the true, intimate history of our evolutions.

In your own individual lives, what areas of growth and development can you identify over the years?

Each of you take time to explain some processes of change in areas of your lives – with the other acting as an interviewer, asking for more detail. The space on the following page can be used to make notes, if needed. Consider the following topics:

- my relationship with my parents
- my political views
- my understanding of myself
- my psychology
- my friendships
- my views on sex
- my behaviour in relationships
- me and my body

We're usefully reminding each other (and ourselves) that we are indeed that most hope-worthy of things: creatures of change.

How have I changed?:

How have I changed?:

33.
Be the Change You Want to See

In our behaviour, we often tend to be making an implicit distinction between two projects: getting other people to change, and changing ourselves. We know we may have to develop in certain ways but, for now, our focus is on altering the other. We make an evolution in our own behaviour conditional on evolutions in other people's. We vow that we'll be nicer if they're nicer, that we'll be less strident if they give up shouting.

However, we're prone to miss an important insight: Changing how you behave to others can be the fastest way to alter how others behave towards you.

People tend – to a remarkable extent – to mirror behaviour. If someone is aggressive around them, they become aggressive back. If someone is gentle, they become soft in return. If someone acts wisely, it'll draw any latent reserves of wisdom out of the audience.

We're often in the paradoxical position of advocating one kind of behaviour while making use of quite another. We might quite angrily suggest that someone else calm down. Or we may bullyingly insist to a person that they try to be more empathetic. We deserve sympathy. It's the agitation and anxiety of trying to teach that can easily take us far from the behaviour we're advocating.

Here it's worth remembering a saying often falsely attributed to Mahatma Gandhi, though eminently useful nevertheless: 'Be the change you want to see'. It captures something key: how sensible it may often be to give up on teaching *directly* in order to try to teach *by example*.

This has one great advantage: We can control ourselves, while it's remarkably hard to exert any sort of direct control over anyone else. Our disappointment with other people should be redirected towards exerting control over the one thing we can reliably command: ourselves.

Seeing us exhibiting certain virtues has a remarkable ability to inspire others into imitating us. And even if change is not immediate, we can at least take pride in the integrity of our position, knowing that we have had the strength and dignity already to have started to become the change we want to see.

How might you change first – independently of any change in your partner – in order to bring about the kind of relationship you want?

34.
Five Questions to Ask of Bad Behaviour

Our partner often behaves rather badly – and when they do, we tend to rush in with some very punitive explanations: They're trying to hurt us; they're deliberately attempting to ruin our lives; they're morons; they've thought long and hard about harming us …

Think of some recent examples of bad behaviour on your partner's part.

Interestingly, small children also sometimes behave in stunningly unfair and horrid ways: They throw stuff on the floor, they scream and say mean things, they try to hit us or steal something from their little brother. But, crucially, our response to this is quite distinctive. We stay calm. We gently sort out the mess. We tend, almost unconsciously, to ask ourselves five key questions:

1.   Might they be tired?
2.   Might they be hungry?
3.   Might they be sad?
4.   Might someone have hurt them?
5.   Might they need a cuddle?

How far we are from behaving like this when we are with fellow adults in general, and our lovers in particular. Here we know at once why they did a bad thing: because they are a terrible person; because they're trying to destroy us; because they're hateful.

But if we employed the infant model of interpretation, we would do something very different. We would, almost unconsciously, before looking elsewhere, ask ourselves the same five key questions:

1.   Might they be tired?
2.   Might they be hungry?
3.   Might they be sad?
4.   Might someone have hurt them?
5.   Might they need a cuddle?

It's very touching that we live in a world where we have learnt to be so kind to children; it would be even nicer if we learnt to be a little more generous towards the child-like parts of one another.

It sounds strange at first – and even condescending – to keep in mind that in crucial ways other adults always remain child-like in part. But this way of seeing a person may be a helpful strategy for managing times when they are very difficult to cope with.

When people fall far short of what we ideally expect from grown-up behaviour and we dismissively label such attitudes as 'childish', without quite realising it we are approaching a hugely constructive idea, but then (understandably though unfortunately) seeing it simply as an accusation, rather than what it truly is: a recognition of an ordinary feature of the human condition.

Adulthood simply isn't a complete state; what we call childhood lasts (in a submerged but significant way) all our lives. Therefore, some of the moves we execute with relative ease around children must forever continue to be relevant when we're dealing with another grown-up.

Being benevolent to another person's inner child doesn't mean infantilising them. It means being charitable in translating things they say in terms of their deeper meaning: 'You're a bastard' might actually be a way of trying to say 'I feel under siege at work and I'm trying to tell myself I'm stronger and more independent than I really feel'.

We'd ideally give more space for soothing rather than arguing; instead of taking our partner up for something annoying they've said, we'd see them like an agitated child who is lashing out at the person they most love because they can't think of what else to do. We'd seek to reassure and show them that they are still OK, rather than (as is so tempting) hit back with equal force.

Of course, it's much, much harder being grown up with another adult whose inner child is on display than it is with an actual child. That's because you can see how little and undeveloped a toddler or a five-year-old is, so sympathy comes naturally. We know it would be a disaster to suddenly turn on the child and try to hold them fully responsible for every moment of their conduct. Psychology has been warning us for half a century or more that this isn't the right route.

We are so alive to the idea that it's patronising to be thought of as younger than we are that we forget that it is also, at times, the greatest privilege for someone to look beyond our adult self in order to engage with – and forgive – the disappointed, furious, inarticulate or wounded child within.

Think again of some recent examples of bad behaviour on your partner's part; imagine that they were, in a certain way, the work of a child. What would it change? How might you have acted differently?

Examples of bad behaviour:

How did you react?

Imagine that they were the work of a child. How might you have acted differently?

35.
Talking About Sex

Sex offers us the single greatest point of emotional connection available in love. But the normal human experience, as relationships progress, is to find sex increasingly difficult. The ideal of spontaneous, passionate sex becomes more and more remote. It's not necessarily that desire diminishes, it's that we become more bewildered and intimidated by each other's sexuality. Our deepening engagement with other aspects of life creates ever less opportunity to access sources of mutual erotic excitement. We tend to discover that our partner becomes, erotically speaking, a stranger to us, the polar opposite of what our culture has led us to expect.

We have to take steps to counteract this tendency, not so much by having more sex (that can be difficult when framed as an immediate command), but by starting to talk more about sex. As a prelude to attempting physical contact, we should get to rediscover the inner workings of our partner's sexual imagination – and share a bit more about our own.

Here are some conversational topics that might help:

A. The past
- Who were the first people you found sexually exciting? When was this? What was it about them?
- How did you learn to masturbate? How did you feel about it?
- What vision of sex was conveyed to you by your parents?
- How did your peer group view sex?
- Did you find any of your parents' friends sexy? What was it about them?
- Try to guess where in your psychological past a major sexual interest of yours comes from.

B. Fantasies

- Describe a typical fantasy you might masturbate to.
- If you could have sex with a complete stranger, what might they be like?
- If you could wave a magic wand, what would you want more of in your sex life?
- Which famous person would you want to sleep with?
- If we decided not to have actual intercourse, but still wanted to do something sexual, what might we get up to?
- I'd like you to believe that my love for you could be compatible with … (name something around sex).

C. Sexiness

- What part of your body do you think is most attractive?
- What sexually hardcore activity would you pick if you had to?
- If you had to start a porn site, what would it be devoted to?
- What kind of clothes turn you on?
- If I was close to orgasm, the thing that would push me over the edge would be if you …

D. Kinkiness

- If sex is more about what's going on in our minds than what's happening to our bodies, what do you find a sexy idea?
- Would you rather degrade or be degraded? And what might you want to do or say?
- In what way do you feel ashamed or guilty around sex?
- If you had to leave your current orientation and have a gay/straight encounter, what would you want your lover to be like?

E. The right mood

A key point about sex is that our mood for it varies hugely. Feeling sexy is not a stable state. There will be occasions when we're feeling flirtatious, confident and wicked, others when we are almost exaggeratedly prim and practical. We are offered a cultural map of what is supposed to make everyone feel sexy, highlighting elements like candlelight, soft music and red wine. These are not ridiculous suggestions, but the map might not be particularly accurate in our own case. If we could accurately identify the factors that work for us, we'd be less dependent on chance – we'd know how to more reliably seduce one another.

Here are some of the factors that can work for people:

Being lightly touched
in the twelve hours
before sex is attempted

Being allowed to think
of someone else

Hotel rooms

Certain clothes

Encouragement to
say 'bad things'

Pornography

Flirting with
strangers

Ensuring the whole
house is tidy first

Boots

It can be very awkward writing down our own list: The things that get us to feel alluring and excited might not be very well aligned with our normal character, so our partner might be a bit surprised. Fortunately we're both confronting the same fears at the same time.

Make your lists separately. You might even each write one thing in sequence, so you are each only making one small revelation at a time.

Things that make me feel sexy:

1.

1.

2.

2.

3.

3.

4.

4.

5.

5.

36.
The Sensate Focus Method

It's so easy, in a couple, to get stuck in a position of not having much sex. Often we stop trying because of something that goes a bit wrong. Perhaps there were some nasty arguments, or moments of impotence, or some kind of awkwardness or discomfort. But what's worse is that failure in the past puts us off from ever really trying again. We become avoidant and shy around the whole topic. One way to break the deadlock is a technique called Sensate Focus, pioneered in the 1980s by the legendary American sex researchers William Masters and Virginia Johnson.

First, stop all attempts to have sex. The idea is that what's stopping good sex is fear; therefore you have to reduce any tension and expectations by rewinding sexual intimacy to its very beginnings.

So, one night, focus wholeheartedly just on one thing: kissing. You can be as passionate as you like, but there should be nothing more. You can press against each other, but there's no nakedness. It's like being back at school, making out, with all the accumulated excitement. Oddly, not being allowed to have sex is pretty erotic.

Then, on another night, you can go a bit beyond kissing, but not a whole lot more. It's like being back on an early date. You can touch bodies, but not really genitals or breasts.

○ ○ ○

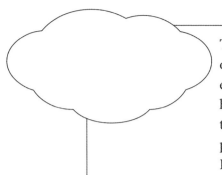

That's for the next time, by which occasion, you'll probably be pretty excited. Again, you can do lots of heavy petting and making out, but this time you can go further – and pleasure and bring each other off. But no more.

That's for the next stage of the Sensate Focus method, when at last you're allowed penetration, but again – with a bow to adolescent sex – only for a moment, and with no expectation of orgasm.

You do
that on a couple more
evenings, and then, hopefully, you can go all the
way, and you should be back to normal sex – though at the slightest
hint of difficulties, just take it back a stage.

37.
Accepting the Problems

The comparatively small number of relationships that endure over a long time and are broadly satisfying for both partners are rarely problem free. But, distinctively, these good enough couples have made an important move: They have come to accept that certain problems between them won't be put right. Ever.

There's enough that's good in the relationship that they can bear to live with a few key areas where they are irreconcilably at odds. When such people talk about their relationship, they say things like:

> We go on separate holidays. My partner loves going to archaeological sites and being very active and I just want to relax on a beach.

> We have separate bedrooms. It's not my ideal, but I'm a very light sleeper and I'd get woken by my partner snoring.

> My partner and I have very opposed (and quite strongly held) political views. We've long since given up trying to persuade each other.

> Nowadays my partner never engages with my family. I wish we could all be together, but they just don't get on.

> My partner's obsessed with clothes and I just want to dress in any way that's comfortable for me. There's constant low-level irritation at what the other chooses to wear. I can't see it changing – but it doesn't seem worth splitting up over now.

> For years we've more or less kept our finances separate; it's very annoying in some ways, but I just couldn't cope with my partner having access to my bank statements and checking everything.

> We haven't had sex for about five years (we're in our sixties). Sometimes it makes me feel very sad, but trying to have sex used to be the cause of endless frustration for both of us.

With such examples in mind, undertake a bold thought experiment. We understand that, until now, the emphasis has been on change, transformation and improvement (there is a firm role for all of these), but try to imagine the opposite: a lack of change, a stubborn resistance to improvement …

Discuss the following:

What conflicts in your relationship do you think you might be able to live with, even if they were never resolved?

What kinds of compromise might you be able to arrive at?

How could it be OK and yet not, substantially, really that different?

38.
Less Pressure on Love

It can feel very weird, and a bit threatening, to talk about taking the pressure off a relationship. Our collective, inherited Romantic culture likes to imagine functioning couples doing more or less everything together and being the meaning of each other's lives. The good couple is, we are told, one in which two people mean more or less everything to one another.

In a sound relationship, we are supposed to meet each other's needs in every area of existence – from sex to intellectual stimulation, cooking styles to bedroom habits. We're supposed to lead our social life in tandem, be the primary sounding board for one another's problems and complete each other in spirit and in matter. If they're involved in a sport, we should at once join in or at least come and support them every weekend; if we want to visit a particular country, they are supposed to come along enthusiastically; our friends are meant to be their friends …

It sounds sweet but it is – over the long term – a recipe for disaster. No two people can ever match each other across all areas of existence, and the attempt to do so inevitably ushers in bitterness and rage. We have, at the collective level, given ourselves a hugely unhelpful picture of how love should go. Any independent move is read like a sign that we can't actually love one another. It is taken to be a sign of imminent danger if we visit other countries on our own or sleep apart. So we end up badgering each other to do things that we don't really like (we force each other to endure tedious hobbies or see each other's peculiar old friends), not even because we inherently want to do this, but because any other arrangement has been predetermined as evidence of betrayal.

A more realistic and, in the proper sense, Romantic view of couples would suggest that there have to be a few strong areas where we can meet each other's needs, but that there should also be plenty of others where we are clearly better off pursuing our goals on our own.

Consider the following list of independent activities and give them a score out of five (one being the least relevant and five being the most relevant):

I'd like to ...	Score out of five:	
travel without my partner		
have dinner one-to-one with a friend		
be able to go to a party without my partner and not have them feel left out		
visit my parents alone		
have my own financial adviser		
go for long walks on my own		
have a separate bathroom		
go shopping with a friend rather than with my partner		

List anything else that comes to mind:

Look at each other's scores and lists. Is there anything that you feel you could accommodate? What might be tricky, and why?

We should recognise that a degree of independence isn't an attack on a partner, it's a guarantee of the solidity of the underlying commitment one has made. Truly stable couples aren't those that do everything together, they are those that have managed to interpret their differences in non-dramatic, non-disloyal terms.

Ultimately a reduction of dependence doesn't mean a relationship is unravelling, it means that we have learnt to focus more clearly and intently on what the other person can actually bring us and have stopped blaming them for not being someone they never were. We no longer need to be upset that their holiday destination strikes us as unrelaxing or that their friends seem boring. We have learnt, instead, to value them for the areas where we truly see eye to eye.

To enjoy a harmonious union with someone, we should ensure that we have plenty of sources of excitement, reassurance and stimulation outside of them. When we hit problems, we should be able to lean on other supports. The demand that another person compensate us for all that's alarming, wearing or deficient in our lives is a mechanism for systematically destroying any relationship. Our conflicts and disappointments will at once feel more manageable when we stop asking our partner to function as our long-lost other half. The more we can survive without the relationship, the greater will be its chances of survival and fulfilment. We will truly give love a chance when we stop wanting it to be everything.

Conclusion

Many congratulations for making it through this book. We hope that – in a variety of small and large ways – the exercises here will make it easier for you to live alongside one another in relative harmony. To conclude, we have drawn up a list of criteria we feel mark out couples who have truly understood what relationships require – and are therefore properly ready for love.

We will be ready for love when …

1. *We have given up on perfection*
When we recognise that we are a flawed species and that whomever we got together with would be radically imperfect in a host of deeply serious ways. We must conclusively kill the idea that things would be ideal with any creature in this galaxy. There can only ever be a 'good enough' relationship.

For this realisation to sink in, it helps to have had a number of relationships before settling down, not in order to have the chance to locate 'the right person', but so that we can have ample opportunity to discover at first hand, in many different contexts, the truth that everyone (even the most initially exciting prospect) really is a bit wrong close up.

2. *We despair of being understood*
Love starts with the experience of being understood in a deeply supportive and uncommon way. They understand the lonely parts of you; they grasp who you truly are. This will not continue. There will always be large tracts of our psyche that remain incomprehensible to anyone else.

We shouldn't blame our lovers for a dereliction of duty in failing to interpret and grasp our internal workings. They were not tragically inept. They simply couldn't understand who we were and what we needed – which is entirely normal. No one properly understands, and can therefore fully sympathise with, anyone else.

3.   *We realise we are crazy*

This is deeply counter-intuitive. We seem so normal and mostly so good. It's the others …

But maturity is founded on an active sense of our own folly. We are out of control for long periods; we have failed to master our past; we make unhelpful 'transferences', we are permanently anxious. We are, at best, a loveable idiot.

If we are not regularly and very deeply embarrassed about who we are, it can only be because we have a dangerous capacity for selective memory.

4.   *We are happy to be taught and calm about teaching*

We are ready for love when we accept that, in certain very significant areas, our partner will be wiser, more reasonable and more mature than we are. We should want to learn from them. We should bear having things pointed out to us. We should, at key points, see them as the teacher and ourselves as pupils. At the same time, we should be ready to take on the task of teaching them certain things and, like good teachers, not shout, lose our tempers or expect them simply to know. Relationships should be recognised as involving a process of mutual education.

5.   *We realise we're not compatible*

The Romantic view of love stresses that the 'right' person means someone who shares our tastes, interests and general attitudes to life. This might be true in the short term, but, over an extended period of time, the relevance of this fades dramatically because differences inevitably emerge. The person who is truly best suited to us is not the person who shares our every taste but the person who can negotiate differences in taste intelligently and wisely; the person who is good at disagreement.

Rather than some notional idea of perfect complementarity, it is the capacity to tolerate difference that is the true marker of the 'right' person. Compatibility is an achievement of love; it must not be its precondition.

Image Credits

p. 17
Gustav Klimt, *The Kiss*, 1907–1908.
Oil on canvas, 180cm × 180cm.
Österreichische Galerie Belvedere, Vienna.

p. 20 [detail]
Albrecht Dürer, *The Rhinoceros*, 1515.
Woodcut, 23.5cm × 29.8cm,
National Gallery of Art, Washington.

p. 22
Niels Christian Kierkegaard, *Unfinished
sketch of Søren Kierkegaard*, circa 1840.
The Royal Library, Denmark.

p. 25
Hugues Merle, *Maternal Affection*, 1867.
Oil on canvas, 100.9cm × 81.2cm.
Private collection.

p. 97
Jacques-Louis David, *Portrait of the
Comtesse Vilain XIIII and her Daughter*,
1816. Oil on canvas, 95cm × 76cm.
National Gallery, London.

p. 100
Claude Monet, *Bazille and Camille (Study
for "Déjeuner sur l'Herbe")*, 1865. Oil on
canvas, 93cm × 68.9cm. National Gallery
of Art, Washington D.C.

p. 152
Jean-Baptiste-Camille Corot, *The Boatman
of Mortefontaine*, 1865–1870. Oil on canvas,
60.9cm × 89.8cm. The Frick Collection,
New York. Henry Clay Frick Bequest.

The School of Life is a global organisation helping people lead more fulfilled lives. It is a resource for helping us understand ourselves, for improving our relationships, our careers and our social lives – as well as for helping us find calm and get more out of our leisure hours. We do this through films, workshops, books, gifts and community. You can find us online, in stores and in welcoming spaces around the globe.